Genesis Chapter 15 Study Aid

A WALK THROUGH THE BIBLE

Davie Smith

New Harbor Press
RAPID CITY, SD

Copyright © 2022 by Davie Smith.

All rights reserved. No part of this publication may be reproduced, distributed or transmitted in any form or by any means, including photocopying, recording, or other electronic or mechanical methods, without the prior written permission of the publisher, except in the case of brief quotations embodied in critical reviews and certain other noncommercial uses permitted by copyright law. For permission requests, write to the publisher, addressed "Attention: Permissions Coordinator," at the address below.

Smith/New Harbor Press
1601 Mt. Rushmore Rd, Ste 3288
Rapid City, SD 57701
www.NewHarborPress.com

Ordering Information:
Quantity sales. Special discounts are available on quantity purchases by corporations, associations, and others. For details, contact the "Special Sales Department" at the address above.

Genesis 15 Study Aid/Davie Smith. —1st ed.
ISBN 978-1-63357-428-1

Acknowledgments

I want to thank my wife, Shirley Smith, and CAPT. Mark Simpson (Ret.) for reviewing this book. This book would not have been possible if it was not for God using these two people.

Contents

Acknowledgments iii
Introduction 1
Chapter 1: Key Lessons 3
Chapter 2: Background 7
    The Timeline 7
    The Key Events Leading Up to Chapter 15 7
Chapter 3: Chapter 15 Overview 11
Chapter 4: The "LORD" in Genesis 15:1 15
    The Translation Pattern for "LORD" 15
    The Grammar of "LORD" 16
    The First Use of "LORD" 17
    "God," "LORD God," and the LORD 18
Chapter 5: The LORD Came in a Vision 19
    The "LORD God" Is "God the Son," Is "Jesus" 19
        Point One: Father Is Creator, Jesus Is Maker 20
        Point Two: Comparing "LORD God" to Jesus 24
        Point Three: "Covenant of Redemption" 25
    God the Father Names Jesus JEHOVAH 32

    John the Baptist Knows Jesus as JEHOVAH 32
    The Pattern of "JEHOVAH" Plus an Adjective 33
Chapter 6: First Use of a Vision by the "LORD" 35
Chapter 7: Jesus Is Our "Shield" and "Reward" 37
    The Promise of Protection to Isaac and Jacob 38
        The Promise of Protection to Isaac 38
        The Promise of Protection to Jacob 39
        The Promise of Protection to All Disciples 39
    Tempting the LORD 40
        Jesus Does Not Tempt His Father 41
        Joseph Does Not Tempt the LORD 42
        David Does Not Tempt the LORD 43
Chapter 8: The "Lord GOD" in Genesis 15:2 45
Chapter 9: "Covenant of Promise" Anxieties 47
    The Response to Abram's Anxieties 48
    The Two Stipulations 49
        The Faith Stipulation 49
        The Exclusivity Stipulation 58
Chapter 10: Reconciling Genesis and Exodus 67
    JEHOVAH Is God's Surname 68
        Israel Is a Surname 68
        Adam Is a Surname 69
        The JEHOVAH Surname in Isaiah 70
        The JEHOVAH Surname in Jeremiah 70

- All Three Have the Surname JEHOVAH 71
- Moses, the Patriarchs, and God's Name 74
  - Moses 74
  - The Patriarchs 74
- The Son Is Separate but Equal to the Father 75

Chapter 11: The Promised Land 81

- The "Promised Land" Comes First 81
- The "Promised Land" and "Rights of Sonship" 82
  - Requirements for Sonship 82
  - Women, Not Members of the Covenants 84
  - God Made Allowances for Strangers 85
- The Casting Out of the "Promised Land" 86
  - Token of Dwelling Ends with the Covenant 86
  - New Dwelling and Individual Tokens 88
  - The New Jerusalem 90

Chapter 12: Response to Promised Land Anxiety 95

- The Animals 96
- The Dividing of the Animals 98

Chapter 13: The First Birth Event 99

Chapter 14: The Abram-Abraham Allegory 101

Chapter 15: The Second Birth Event 103

- The Roles of the Cast of Characters 103
- Mount Sinai is a Type of Wedding Ceremony 108
  - The Characters and the Process 108

The New Testament Meaning............................109
Chapter 16: The Name Change 115
  Repeating and Expanding (Telescoping) 118
  The Overall Symbolism 121
Chapter 17: Forerunner Similarities.............................123
  They Were Pursued and Persecuted 127
  Many Are Called, But Few Are Chosen 130
Chapter 18: Numbering the Children of Israel 137
  Numbered after the Exodus 137
  The "Numbered" Produced the Innumerable.........139
  Numbered Producing Innumerable Repeated 141
  David Angers the LORD by Counting Israel...........143
  Numbered Twice after the Exodus 145
  The Spiritual Bondage of God's People 146
Chapter 19: Driving Away the Fowls............................149
  The Fowls Came..149
  Moses Waited and Waved Off the Fowls.................151
    The LORD Orchestrates Scenarios 151
    Waving Off Noise and Waiting On the LORD ...154
  David Waited On the LORD.....................................155
    The Fowls and the Battle of Good versus Evil ...156
    Returning Good for Evil...157
    Wait On the LORD, Evildoers Are Cut Down....158
Chapter 20: Servitude to Great Substance...................161

    The LORD Prophesied the Pattern............................ 161

    The 400-Year Span from Isaac to the Exodus......... 162

    The Pattern Began with Isaac.................................... 163

    The Pattern Continued with Jacob............................ 164

    The Pattern Continued with the Twelve 166

Chapter 21: But in the Fourth Generation.................... 169

Chapter 22: Other Related Timespans 171

    Exodus 6:16–20.. 171

    Exodus 12:40–41.. 172

    Galatians 3:17 175

    1 Kings 6:1 and Acts 13:17–21.................................... 179

Chapter 23: The Amorites' Iniquity Not Yet Full....... 181

    The Three Salient Points 181

        The Timeline for the Promised Land 182

        Abram's Seed, An Instrument for Judgment 183

        A Timeline for Judgment.. 184

        Comparison to Daniel's "70-Week" Prophecy ... 185

Chapter 24: Cutting the Blood Covenant..................... 191

    The Smoking Furnace and the Burning Lamp........ 191

    "God the Father" and Jesus Are at Mount Sinai...... 192

    The Fowls after Cutting the Blood Covenant 195

    A Three-Party "Blood Covenant" 198

Chapter 25: The Promised Land Boundaries 203

Chapter 26: Summary... 205

Appendix I 209
   "Elohim" Is a Title, Not a Name 209
Appendix II 217
   Other Hebrew Words Translated as "Vision" 217
Appendix III 219
   The Symbolism of Heifers in the Bible 219
      The Prophetic Meaning of the Heifer 226
Index of Questions 229

Introduction

The purposes of this book are: (1) to provide a study aid for Genesis chapter 15; (2) to propose answers to questions related to this chapter; and (3) to explain chapter 15 in such a way that readers will see the prophecies in this chapter, the fulfillment of those prophecies in the New Testament (NT),[1] and they will see the consistency of the Holy Scriptures. It neither intends to be the "one true" interpretation of the LORD's Word nor to provide final answers. This study aid is a small step in gaining a better understanding of the LORD's Word.

Though there is one interpretation of the "Word of God," there are many applications. By diligently

---

[1] Drane, John, "BBC - Religions - Christianity: The Bible," https://www.bbc.co.uk/religion/religions/christianity/texts/bible.shtml. Retrieved 20 April 2022.

studying the "Word of God," we may discover applications that will positively affect our behavior and bring us spiritually closer to the LORD. This study aid, therefore, is a journey of discovery, not a destination.

This book shows that the Bible is neither two books, the Old Testament (OT)[2] and the NT, nor is it sixty-six independent books. Each of the sixty-six books in the Bible is dependent on the others to complete and validate each other. Moreover, the OT foretells, and the NT fulfills. This book also shows that the Bible is one book with one inspiring author. However, there were several men, over several centuries, who wrote under the inspiration of this author—the LORD.

---

2 Drane, John, "BBC - Religions - Christianity: The Bible."

CHAPTER 1

Key Lessons

There are, at least, four key lessons in this study aid. **First,** Jesus is the LORD, JEHOVAH, that appears to Abram in a vision in Genesis chapter 15. No other Person in the Trinity[3] manifests Himself in the flesh. Jesus appears to Abram as a Comforter, Protector, and an exceedingly great Reward. He is there when Abram needs Him, and He will be there when we need Him too.

Second, faith is not a lack of anxiety while performing God's mission—anxiety is a natural part of the human nature that God gave us. Faith,

---

3 In this book, the "Trinity" is defined as three divine, but distinct persons: God the Father, God the Son (Jesus), and God the Holy Spirit. These three Persons have the same substance (essence), but Jesus and God the Holy Spirit are subordinate to God the Father.

however, is the demonstration of obedience and perseverance in spite of our anxieties. Our obedience and perseverance serve as evidence of our faith. We must obey and persevere while neither knowing nor understanding "how" God will protect us and fulfill His promises.

Third, we must wave off the fowls sent by Satan to devour our spiritual sacrifices and to destroy our ability to fulfill the LORD's mission. These fowls may be evil attacks that are not meant to destroy us directly, but they are to provoke us to return evil for evil and endanger our relationship with the LORD. Satan wants to use the LORD's love for us as a weapon against the LORD.

We are merely tools for Satan in his battle against the LORD. Satan wants to deceive us into working against our own best interest and into losing our salvation. We cannot let the evil that Satan directs against us through others breed hatred. Hatred can breed sin, sin can lead to spiritual death, and spiritual death is eternal separation from the LORD.

Fourth, the Bible explains why Jesus came, how to recognize Him, and what to expect from Him, His Father, and the Holy Spirit. We should feel confident in who Jesus is, and what He did. This is because the OT tells us what He would do, the NT tells us what He did, and they agree. Jesus tells His followers, "And now I have told you before it come to pass, that, when it is come to pass, ye might believe."[4]

This book shows the consistency within the Holy Scriptures and the linkages between the OT and the NT: the symbols, timelines, prophecies, and covenants. My prayer is that readers leave with a better understanding of the inerrancy of God's Word, the relationship between the OT and the NT, and will either establish or strengthen their relationship with Jesus.

---

4 Jhn. 14:29

CHAPTER 2

Background

The Timeline

Chapter 15 begins 2,026 years after the "LORD God" forms and creates Adam, 370 years after the flood, 78 years after Abram's birth, 68 years after Sarai's birth, and 3 years after God calls Abram in Genesis chapter 12.[5]

The Key Events Leading Up to Chapter 15

The Bible begins focusing on Abram and the LORD's covenant with him in Genesis chapter 12.

---

5 According to Jasher 16:22, Abram is 78 years old when God appears to him in Genesis chapter 15. According to Gen.17:17, Sarai is ten years younger than Abram. According to Gen. 12:4, Abram is 75 years old when God calls him in Genesis chapter 12.

The LORD tells Abram that his part of this covenant, as written in the King James Version (KJV) of the Bible, is to "get thee out of thy country, and from thy kindred, and from thy father's house, unto a land that [the LORD] will shew [him]."[6] Later in chapter 14, we learn that the LORD makes at least one more stipulation, Abram is "not [to] take from [the inhabitants of the land] a thread even to a shoelatchet, and that [he] will not take any thing that is [theirs]."[7]

In return, God promises Abram that He will: (1) make of him a great nation, (2) bless him, (3) make his name great, (4) be a blessing, (5) bless them that bless him, (6) curse him that curseth him, and (7) in thee shall all families of the earth be blessed.[8] Thus, the "Promised Land" is a stipulation and a dwelling place for the people of the "Promises," it is not one of the seven "Promises."

After Abram leaves his country, a famine causes him to sojourn in Egypt. But before entering Egypt, Abram asks his wife Sarai to tell the Pharaoh that she is his sister. Abram does this because Sarai is

---

6 Gen. 12:1
7 Gen. 14:23
8 Gen. 12:2–3

beautiful, and he fears that the Egyptian Pharaoh will kill him to have Sarai as his wife.[9]

Abram's plan appears to work. The Pharaoh takes Sarai to be his wife. And because he believes that Abram is Sarai's brother, he does not take Abram's life. The LORD, however, sends plagues against Egypt and reveals to the Pharaoh that Sarai is Abram's wife. This prompts the Pharaoh to command Abram to "behold thy wife, take her, and go thy way."[10]

After leaving Egypt, Abram deals with resource conflicts "between the herdmen of [his] cattle and the herdmen of Lot's cattle."[11] This conflict emanates from the Pharaoh entreating "Abram well for [Sarai's] sake: and he had sheep, and oxen, and he asses, and menservants, and maidservants, and she asses, and camels."[12] Thus, Abram has more exiting Egypt than he had entering.

Abram resolves these conflicts by separating from Lot. But later in chapter 14, Lot is captured by four kings.[13] Abram then "armed his trained servants, born in his own house, three hundred

---

9 Gen. 12:11–13
10 Gen. 12:19
11 Gen. 13:7
12 Gen. 12:16
13 Gen. 14: 1–12

and eighteen, and he pursued"[14] and successfully fights and rescues Lot from the four Kings.[15] While returning from the battle, Abram communes with and receives a blessing from Melchizedek, king of Salem.[16]

In addition, in chapter 14, we learn that Abram, at some point in time, had lifted "up [his] hand unto the LORD, the most high God, the possessor of heaven and earth, That [he would] not take from [the inhabitants of the land] a thread even to a shoelatchet, and that [he] will not take any thing that is thine."[17] This is a second stipulation for receiving the "Promises" from the LORD. This promise and the seven "Promises" that the LORD makes to Abram are based solely on the LORD's Word and Abram's word. There is no formal carnal covenant cut. The only formal "blood covenant" cut is for the "Promised Land."

---

14 Gen. 14:14
15 Gen. 14:15–16
16 Gen 14:18–20
17 Gen. 14:22–23

CHAPTER 3

Chapter 15 Overview

In Genesis chapter 15, Abram has fulfilled his end of the covenant with the LORD and is waiting on the LORD to fulfill His part. Abram left his country and his kindreds, did not accept anything from the inhabitants, and is in the "Promised Land." The remaining tasks are for the LORD to fulfill. Abram, however, is anxious. He knows "what" the LORD promised, but he lacks an understanding of "how" and "when" the LORD will fulfill His "Promises." This is, in essence, a meaning of "faith"; the believing in the "what" while not understanding the "how" and "when."

The LORD's promises to Abram are twofold: to provide him with land and to make his descendants as "innumerable as the stars." At this point, the land is inhabited by a multitude of people,

Abram is 78-years-old without a child, and his wife, Sarai, is 68-years-old and barren. Abram understands and believes God, but he does not understand "how" and "when" He will fulfill His promises. This causes Abram anxiety. That said, Abram shows faith by aligning his actions and words according to the LORD's promises. He does this while not understanding "how" a 78-year-old man and a 68-year-old barren woman will have offspring as "innumerable as the stars."

The LORD knew Abram's anxieties about the "Promises" related to his "seed" and the "Promised Land." He comforts and reassures Abram of His protection. He addresses Abram's anxieties by (1) confirming His Promises, (2) providing more details, and (3) by giving Abram a partial vision of the future fulfillment of both sets of promises. And, though the LORD follows the same pattern for both sets of promises, there is a notable difference. With the "Promised Land," the LORD cuts a "carnal-blood covenant" with Abram.

The KJV describes the vision of "God the Father," a "smoking furnace," and Jesus, a "burning lamp," cutting a "carnal-blood covenant" with Abram to reassure him that his "seed" will one day receive the "Promised Land."[18] Abram's "seed," however,

---

18 Gen. 15:17

will receive the "Promised Land" after going through a 400-year pattern of being put into servitude for a period of time and then exiting servitude with "great substance." We also note that Abram is an inactive participant in the cutting of this "carnal-blood covenant." After all, he has fulfilled his portion of the covenant. The only unfulfilled promises are those made by the LORD.

CHAPTER 4

The "LORD" in Genesis 15:1

The Translation Pattern for "LORD"

The first sentence in Genesis 15:1 reads, "After these things the word of the LORD came unto Abram in a vision." This is the sixty-second time in the KJV where "LORD" is in all capital letters. The Hebrew word translated "LORD" in the KJV is "יְהֹוָה" (yehôvâh), or JEHOVAH.[19] This translation pattern "is found in most of the English translations that have been produced over the past several centuries. The notable exception is the American Standard Version (1901), which uses the term "Jehovah" rather than "LORD." In these common versions, the translators are attempting to make known to the English readers

---

19 Strong's Concordance H3068

that different Hebrew words were found in the original text."[20]

The Grammar of "LORD"

"LORD" differs from "Lord" and "lord" in the KJV. "LORD" reflects the original term "YHWH" (found 6,823 times in the KJV), which the Jews considered God's name. "Lord" (standard capitalization) is the English rendition of the Hebrew "Adonai." The Jews consider God's name, "YHWH" (four consonants), to be very sacred and do not pronounce His name. "Eventually, the scribes borrowed vowels from the name 'Adonai' based upon a point system, which reflected the way the language was spoken. Vowels were thus inserted into the sacred four-letter name (called the "Tetragrammaton"—"four letters"). This eventually evolved into the hybrid word JEHOVAH around the beginning of the twelfth century AD."[21] (The abbreviation "AD" stands for the Latin phrase "Anno Domini." This Latin phrase means "in the year of [our] Lord."[22])

---

20 Jackson, Wayne. "LORD and Lord: What's the Difference?" ChristianCourier.com. Access date: April 19, 2022. https://www.christiancourier.com/articles/305-lord-and-lord-whats-the-difference.
21 Jackson, Wayne. "LORD and Lord: What's the Difference?"
22 Online Etymology Dictionary, https://www.etymonline.com/word/Anno%20Domini. Retrieved 21 April 2022.

The First Use of "LORD"

From Genesis chapter 2 to chapter 15, "LORD" ("YHWH" or "JEHOVAH") is either used by itself or paired with "God." "God" is the English translation of the Hebrew word "אֱלֹהִים" (Elohim). But, unlike "JEHOVAH," which is God's name, "Elohim" refers to God by a title or as a reference to Him being a deity, not by His name (see Appendix I). Thus, in Genesis chapter 1, "Elohim" identifies the God of creation by a title or that He is a deity—not by His name. This God spoke, or commanded, the creation—He is the creator. He brings into existence something from nothing by saying "let there be: . . . and there was."[23]

Conversely, from Genesis 2:4 to 3:23, the Scriptures use the "LORD God" (JEHOVAH Elohim) pair to declare that the God name JEHOVAH takes what the God in chapter 1 creates and makes man. The "LORD God" in Genesis 2:4 to 3:23 "formed man of the dust of the ground,"[24] He breaths into man a spirit created for him, and man becomes a living soul.[25] Thus, for man to be a "living soul," he must have, simultaneously, a formed body and a created spirit. Consequently, man is both formed and

---

23 Gen. 1:3, 6, 9, 11, 14, 20, 24, Psa. 148:5
24 Gen. 2:7, Jhn. 1:3
25 Gen. 2:7, 5:2; Psa. 104:30

created,[26] and man is both spirit and body. Also, the "LORD God" talks and dwells with Adam and Eve.

"God," "LORD God," and the LORD

These observations provide insight into who the God (Elohim) is in Genesis chapter 1, who the "LORD God" (JEHOVAH Elohim) is in Genesis chapters 2 and 3, and who the "LORD" is in Genesis 15:1. They suggest that the God in Genesis chapter 1 is "God the Father," the "LORD God" in Genesis chapters 2 and 3 is "God the Son," and the "LORD" that appears to Abram in a vision in Genesis 15:1 is also "God the Son," Jesus.

---

26 Gen. 5:1

Chapter 5

The LORD Came in a Vision

The "LORD God" Is "God the Son," Is "Jesus"

The "LORD God" in Genesis chapters 2 and 3 is the Jesus in the four Gospels of the NT. This conclusion is based on three points: (1) the difference between creating and making, (2) the comparison of the "LORD God" in Genesis chapters 2 and 3 with the Jesus in the NT, and (3) the identification of the Establishers of the "Covenant of Redemption"[27] in Genesis chapter 3 and the Fulfiller of the "Covenant of Redemption" in the NT.

---

27 "Covenant Theology." Ligonier Ministries. Accessed April 24, 2022. https://www.ligonier.org/guides/covenant-theology.

Point One: Father Is Creator, Jesus Is Maker
Point one is based on "God the Father" as the Creator, and God the Son, Jesus, as the Maker. This is substantiated by John 1:3 which states, "All things were made by [Jesus]; and without [Jesus] was not any thing made that was made." Thus, all things were "made" by Jesus, not "created" by Jesus. We find potential contradictions to this interpretation of John 1:3 in Colossians 1:16 and in Ephesians 3:9. But, after careful analysis, we discover a translation error and a questionable addition to the Holy Scriptures.

Colossians 1:16: The KJV translates the Greek word "ἐν" (en) as "by" in Colossians 1:16. This identifies Jesus as the agent performing the action. However, according to Strong's Concordance, this Greek word is "a primary preposition denoting (fixed) position (in place, time or state),"[28] not a word that identifies an agent performing an action. The Greek word that is translated as "by" to identify an agent performing an action is "διά" (dia), and this Greek word is used in John 1:3 to show that Jesus is the agent that made all things.[29] Hence, if "by" is used as a preposition to show

---

28 Strong's Concordance G1722
29 Strong's Concordance G1223

proximity, such as "standing *by* the window,"[30] it would be accurate—but it is not used that way. Consequently, "by" is not an accurate translation.

The context of Colossians 1:16 manifests in the verses immediately before and after. Verses 15 and 17 declare the timing of creation, and they both depict the timing relative to Jesus and His existence. Verse 15 reads, "Who is the image of the invisible God, the firstborn of every creature." Verse 17 reads, "And he is before all things, and by him all things consist." The context of these verses is not about identifying Jesus as the One who performed creation. Instead, it is about declaring the timing of creation as occurring **after** Jesus.

The Greek word "ἐν" should not be translated as "by" to identify Jesus as the agent performing creation. Instead, the word that best fits the context of Colossians 1:16 is "**after**" to identify that "**after** [Jesus] were all things created, that are in heaven, and that are in earth, visible and invisible, whether they be thrones, or dominions, or principalities, or powers: all things were created **after** [Jesus], and for [Jesus]." So, "God the Father"

---

30 "By." Merriam-Webster. Accessed April 24, 2022. https://www.merriam-webster.com/dictionary/by.

creates all things for His Son, Jesus, who existed before creation.

So, no inconsistency exists between John 1:3 and Colossians 1:16. However, there is a translation error in Colossians 1:16. Moreover, the review of Genesis chapters 1–3, John 1:3, and Colossians 1:16 provides more evidence that "God the Father," the "Elohim" of Genesis chapter 1, created; that Jesus, the "LORD God" of Genesis chapters 2 and 3, made; that Jesus is the "LORD God" of Genesis chapters 2 and 3; and, that Jesus is before all creation.

Ephesians 3:9: This verse reads, "And to make all men see what is the fellowship of the mystery, which from the beginning of the world hath been hid in God, who created all things by Jesus Christ." The translators of the KJV may have inserted the phrase "by Jesus Christ." This is noted in a couple of well-known commentaries. In the John Gill commentary on this verse, he states, "The phrase, 'by Jesus Christ,' is left out in the Alexandrian and Claromontane copies, and in the Vulgate Latin, Syriac, and Ethiopic versions."

The insertion of this phrase is also noted in Albert Barnes' commentary. It says, "There is a striking resemblance between the passage and that in Col

1:15–16. But the phrase is missing in the Vulgate, the Syriac, the Coptic, and in several of the ancient [manuscripts]. Mill remarks that it was probably inserted here by some transcriber from the parallel passage in Col 1:16; and it is rejected as an interpolation by Griesbach." Barnes adds the comment that "it is not 'very' material whether it be retained in this place or not, as the same sentiment is elsewhere abundantly taught; see Joh 1:3; Col 1:16; Heb 1:2." Yet, this is "material" because of the issue just raised in Colossians 1:16 and that the word used in Hebrews 1:2 is "made."

The KJV makes a distinction between "made" and "created." "Created" is used twelve times in the NT, and it is translated from the same Greek word each time, "κτίζω." This Greek word is used fourteen times in the NT. It is translated as "created" twelve times, "Creator" once, and "make" once. The one time that this Greek word is translated as "make" is in Ephesians 2:15.

Ephesians 2:15 reads, "Having abolished in his flesh the enmity, even the law of commandments contained in ordinances; for to **make** in himself of twain one new man, so making peace." Even in this verse, "create" may be a more appropriate choice of an English word. Interestingly, the Greek word normally translated as "make" is not used in this verse. This Greek word is the same Greek word that is translated as "made" in John 1:3, "γίνομαι," and it is used 672 times in the NT; it is never translated as "created," it is translated as "made" over 650 times in the NT.

There is persuasive evidence of the insertion of "by Jesus Christ" to the end of Ephesians 3:9. The evidence is the absence of this phrase in other manuscripts, the consistent translations of the two Greek words for "made" and "created," and the distinction made between the word "made" and "created." By removing this questionable phrase, John 1:3 reconciles with Colossians 1:16, Ephesians 3:9, and Hebrews 1:2. Thus, Ephesians 3:9 should read: "And to make all men see what is the fellowship of the mystery, which from the beginning of the world hath been hid in God, who created all things."

Point Two: Comparing "LORD God" to Jesus
The second point is based on comparing what the "LORD God" does in the Garden of Eden to what Jesus does in the NT. In chapters 2 and 3, the "LORD God" dwells, walks, and speaks with Adam and Eve.[31] And after Adam and Eve sin, He

---

31 Gen. 3:9–19

makes a covenant to redeem Adam and Eve and their future seed from their fallen state.[32]

There are significant similarities between the "LORD God" in the Garden of Eden and the Jesus in the NT. The "LORD God" in the Garden of Eden and Jesus manifest Themselves in the flesh to man, They dwell with man, They shape and comfort man, and They both are tied to the "Covenant of Redemption"—one establishes it and the other fulfills it. Moreover, Jesus is the only person of the Trinity that mankind, at any time, has seen or touched.[33] Thus, the "LORD God" that is in the Garden of Eden and the "LORD" that appears to Abram in a vision in Genesis 15:1 is the Jesus in the NT.

Point Three: "Covenant of Redemption"
The Origin of the "Covenant of Redemption": The God in Genesis chapter 1 establishes a covenant with Adam. He tells Adam to "be fruitful, and multiply, and replenish the earth, and subdue it: and have dominion over the fish of the sea, and over the fowl of the air, and over every living thing that moveth upon the earth. And God said, Behold, I have given you every herb bearing seed, which is upon the face of all the earth, and

---

32 Gen. 3:9–24, Jhn. 17:1–5, Rev. 13:8, 1 Jhn. 3:8
33 Jhn. 1:18, 1 Jhn. 4:12, 1 Tim. 6:15–16

every tree, in the which is the fruit of a tree yielding seed; to you it shall be for meat. And to every beast of the earth, and to every fowl of the air, and to every thing that creepeth upon the earth, wherein there is life, I have given every green herb for meat: and it was so."[34]

This was a covenant of stewardship. God gives Adam stewardship over the earth and over all that is within the earth. Moreover, God "blessed the seventh day, and sanctified it: because that in it he had rested from all his work which God created and made."[35] The keeping of the "seventh day is a token, or an ordinance, for this covenant. But, interestingly, this ordinance is referred to as the "seventh day," not the "Sabbath Day."

The ordinance of the "Sabbath Day" is not introduced in the KJV until Exodus 16:23, the LORD "said unto them, This is that which the LORD hath said, To morrow is the rest of the holy sabbath unto the LORD: bake that which ye will bake to day, and seethe that ye will seethe; and that which remaineth over lay up for you to be kept until the morning."[36] This reference comes after

---

34 Gen. 1:28–30
35 Gen. 2:3
36 Exo. 16:23

the exodus but before the establishment of the "Old Covenant."

Thus, we have, what appears to be, the same type of ordinance introduced twice over a 2,500-year period. Moreover, after the LORD introduces the "seventh day," He does not refer to it again until 2,500 years later. But when He does, it has a new name. This is an interesting observation, but it is beyond the scope of this book. Therefore, this observation will not be explored any further.

In Genesis chapter 2, the "LORD God" builds upon, but does not replace, the covenant from Genesis chapter 1. He adds to it a token of dwelling[37] called the "Garden of Eden" and a stipulation for dwelling in the Garden of Eden. "The LORD God planted a garden eastward in Eden; and there he put the man whom he had formed. And out of the ground made the LORD God to grow every tree that is pleasant to the sight, and good for food; the tree of life also in the midst of the garden, and the tree of knowledge of good and evil."[38] The "LORD God" stipulates to Adam that "of every tree of the garden thou mayest freely eat: But of the tree of the knowledge of good and evil, thou shalt not eat

---

[37] A "Token of Dwelling" in this book refers to a place set aside for covenant members, only, to dwell.
[38] Gen. 2:8–9

of it: for in the day that thou eatest thereof thou shalt surely die."[39] This subcovenant is referred to in this book as the "Adamic Covenant."

After establishing the "Adamic Covenant," the "LORD God" dwells, walks, and talks with Adam and Eve.[40] But, after Adam sins and breaks the "Adamic Covenant" with Him and with the God in Genesis chapter 1, they no longer have a right to dwell in the Garden of Eden. Consequently, the "LORD God" casts both Adam and Eve out of the Garden of Eden, and He makes a new covenant.

This new covenant is called the "Covenant of Redemption," and it is with the God in Genesis chapter 1 and the "LORD God" in Genesis chapters 2 and 3. The purpose of the "Covenant of Redemption" is to redeem Adam and Eve and their future seed from their fallen state.[41] And, because the previous covenant is broken, the "Covenant of Redemption" replaces the "Adamic Covenant," and, it replaces the Garden of Eden as a carnal token of dwelling with a future spiritual token of dwelling called "New Jerusalem."

---

[39] Gen. 2:16–17
[40] Gen. 3:9–19
[41] Gen. 3:9–24, Jhn. 17:1–5, 1 Jhn. 3:8, Rev. 13:8

A Male Lamb without Spot or Blemish: After the "LORD God" establishes the "Covenant of Redemption," He sets the ritual-substitutional sacrifice of a male lamb without spot or blemish as an ordinance for the covenant. This is "the Lamb slain from the foundation of the world"[42] as a substitutional sacrifice for Adam and Eve after they sinned.[43] This is the lamb that the "LORD God" slays to make "coats of skins, and clothed"[44] Adam and Eve. This is the lamb offered by Abel that the LORD respects.[45] This is the lamb that Abraham offers instead of Isaac,[46] and this is the lamb that is sacrificed in the place of the firstborn in the houses that has its blood "on the two side posts and on the upper door post"[47] in Egypt.

Moreover, the ritual-substitutional sacrifice of a male lamb without blemish is an ordinance used to identify God's people. The LORD tells His people that they are to keep "a feast to the LORD throughout your generations; ye shall keep it a feast by an ordinance for ever."[48] The LORD calls this ordinance "the ordinance of the Passover: There shall

---

42 Rev. 13:8
43 Gen. 3:21
44 Gen. 3:21
45 Gen. 4:4
46 Gen. 22:13
47 Exo. 12:7
48 Gen. 12:14

no stranger eat thereof: But every man's servant that is bought for money, when thou hast circumcised him, then shall he eat thereof. A foreigner and an hired servant shall not eat thereof."[49]

Jesus Fulfills the "Covenant of Redemption": This ritual-substitutional sacrifice of a male lamb without blemish starts in the Garden of Eden. This ordinance is kept by God's people in both the OT and the NT until Jesus fulfills the "Covenant of Redemption." Jesus fulfills this covenant by dying on "Passover"[50] and His Father resurrecting Him from the dead on the "Feast of Firstfruits."[51,52] Hence, the ordinances that the LORD establishes under the "Covenant of Promise" and the "Old Covenant" all pointed to the fulfillment of the "Covenant of Redemption" by Jesus.

Jesus fulfills the "Noahic Covenant" ordinance by walking upon the earth under the Rainbow. Jesus fulfills the "Covenant of Promise"[53] ordinances

---

49 Gen. 12:43–45

50 Jhn. 19:31 (Passover is also the Preparation Day for the first day of the "Feast of Unleavened Bread," which is treated as a Sabbath.)

51 Lev. 23: 9–14; Matt. 28:1–10; 1 Cor. 15:21–23; Col. 1:18; Rev. 1:5, 14:1–5

52 Acts 2:24, Gal. 1:1, Rom. 10:9, Heb. 13:20

53 Gen. 12:1–3

by being circumcised[54] on the eighth day.[55] Jesus fulfills the "Old Covenant" ordinances by keeping the daily and monthly sacrifices, the Sabbaths, and the LORD's "Appointed Days." Jesus fulfills the "Covenant of Water Baptism"[56] ordinance by being baptized by John the Baptist in the Jordan River.[57] Moreover, Jesus establishes and fulfills the "New Covenant" ordinances by establishing and participating in the "Communion"[58,59] and in the "Washing of the Saints' Feet."[60] Lastly, Jesus fulfills the "New Covenant" ordinances by accepting the "Holy Spirit."[61]

However, to fulfill the "Covenant of Redemption," Jesus takes on the form of a man with a living soul.[62] His body is formed of the dust of the ground and contains a spirit.[63] To elaborate, Jesus' body is formed within Mary, but is "of the dust of the ground." The spirit within His body is His

---

54 Gen. 17:10–14
55 Luk. 2:21
56 Mar. 1:4; Luk. 3:3; Acts 1:22, 13:24, 19:4
57 Matt. 3:13–17
58 Luk. 22:14–23; Jhn. 13:1–30
59 "Communion." Merriam-Webster. Merriam-Webster. Accessed April 24, 2022. https://www.merriam-webster.com/dictionary/communion.
60 Jhn. 13:1–20
61 Matt. 4:1; Luk. 4:1
62 Rom. 8:3, Jhn. 1:14, 1 Tim. 3:16
63 Gen. 2:7

Spirit, and It "is conceived in her . . . of the Holy Ghost."[64] Jesus' Spirit is in the beginning and is for eternity. Consequently, when Jesus offers up His carnal body as a substitutional sacrifice to fulfill the "Covenant of Redemption," His Spirit departs His body, returns on the "third day," and lives for eternity.

God the Father Names Jesus JEHOVAH

John the Baptist Knows Jesus as JEHOVAH

When John the Baptist sees "Jesus coming unto him, and [he] saith, Behold the Lamb of God, which taketh away the sin of the world,"[65] he knows that Jesus is the one spoken of in Isaiah 40:3 as well as Malachi 3:1 and 4:5–6. John the Baptist says, "I am the voice of one crying in the wilderness, Make straight the way of the Lord."[66] He knows Jesus by His "God the Father" given name, JEHOVAH. We know this because John the Baptist says that he is the one "that crieth in the wilderness, Prepare ye the way of the LORD (JEHOVAH)."[67]

---

64 Matt. 1:20
65 Jhn. 1:29
66 Jhn. 1:23
67 Isa. 40:3

Thus, John the Baptist knows that he is preparing the way for JEHOVAH, and this is Jesus. This is the same JEHOVAH, or Jesus, that is in Genesis chapters 2 and 3; this is the JEHOVAH, or Jesus, that appears to Abram in Genesis 15:1; and, this is the JEHOVAH, or Jesus, Isaiah refers to in Isaiah 40:3.

The Pattern of "JEHOVAH" Plus an Adjective
Confirmation that Jesus' name is JEHOVAH is also found in His Hebrew name, "יְעוּשׁוֹהִ" (Jehoshua), which means JEHOVAH-saved.[68] Hence, JEHOVAH is Jesus' Hebrew name, and "saved" is an adjective that describes what He did when He came in the flesh and offered Himself as a substitutional sacrifice so "that the world through him might be saved."[69]

The joining of "JEHOVAH" to an adjective to describe something He did is also found in the OT. We find "Jehovah-jireh," or "JEHOVAH-Provide," in Genesis 22:14. "JEHOVAH-Provide" is not Jesus' name. JEHOVAH is His name; "Provide" is an adjective describing what He did in providing a ram-lamb as a substitutional sacrifice for Isaac.[70]

---

68 Strong Concordance H3091
69 Jhn. 3:17
70 The assertion that JEHOVAH-Jireh refers to Jesus is based on the interpretation of Exodus 6:3 that Abraham only knew

"Jehovah-nissi," or "JEHOVAH-Banner," is found in Exodus 17:15. "JEHOVAH-Banner" is not Jesus' name. JEHOVAH is His name; "Banner" is an adjective describing what He did in using the raised hands of Moses as a banner to defeat Amalek.[71] This is reminiscent of the banner, or standard, of Jesus' outstretched arms on the cross to gain strength in our fight to defeat Satan and to identify places for us to gather and worship God.

When the Hebrews encamped in the wilderness, they are in groups according to their tribes and are identified by the banners, or standards, of their tribes. Each tribe has a banner, or standard, which specifies where they will gather and encamp.[72] Similarly, today Christian churches use the banner of the cross to identify their buildings as places for Christians to gather and worship.

God the Son by JEHOVAH, and he did not know God the Father by JEHOVAH.
71 Exo. 17:8–14
72 Num. 2

CHAPTER 6

First Use of a Vision by the "LORD"

The only time that the Hebrew word for "vision" is translated in the KJV of Genesis, Exodus, and Leviticus is in Genesis 15:1. This Hebrew word "הָמַחֲזֶ" (makh-az-eh') occurs only four times in four OT verses. It means "vision (in the ecstatic state)."[73] Thus, Abram's vision in Genesis 15:1 brings him a feeling of great joy and encouragement, and he may have been in an ecstatic state and in "*a trance, but having his eyes open.*"[74]

There are five other Hebrew words for "vision" in the KJV (see Appendix II). "Vision" first appears

---

73 Strong's Concordance, H4236; Gen. 15:1; Num. 24:4, 16; Eze. 13:7
74 Num. 24:4, 16

in Genesis 15:1, and one may conclude that this is perhaps the first time that JEHOVAH appears to man in a vision. Thus, before Genesis 15:1, JEHOVAH, Jesus, may communicate only in the flesh or only audibly with man. This observation provides more circumstantial evidence that JEHOVAH, Jesus, is in the flesh in the Garden of Eden; in the flesh when He "came down to see the city and the tower, which the children of men builded"[75]; and, He is in the flesh when He "appeared unto Abram"[76] in Genesis chapter 12.

---

75 Gen. 11:5
76 Gen. 12:7

Chapter 7

Jesus Is Our "Shield" and "Reward"

The LORD tells Abram in the last clause of Genesis 15:1 that He is his "shield, and [his] exceeding great reward." The LORD's promises come with an inherent promise of a "shield" of protection "until [He has] done *that* which [He has] spoken to thee of."[77] The LORD extends His promise of a "shield" of protection to Isaac, to Jacob, and to all His earthly-fathered "Sons of Promises." Furthermore, this "shield" of protection covers all Holy Ghost-filled Disciples of Jesus.[78]

---

77 Gen. 28:15
78 Matt. 28: 20

The Promise of Protection to Isaac and Jacob

The Promise of Protection to Isaac

In Genesis chapter 26, "Isaac went unto Abimelech king of the Philistines unto Gerar. And the LORD appeared unto [Isaac], and said, Go not down into Egypt; dwell in the land which I shall tell thee of: Sojourn in this land, and I will be with thee, and will bless thee; for unto thee, and unto thy seed, I will give all these countries, and I will perform the oath which I sware unto Abraham thy father."[79]

The LORD also tells Isaac that He "will make thy seed to multiply as the stars of heaven, and will give unto thy seed all these countries; and in thy seed shall all the nations of the earth be blessed; Because that Abraham[80] obeyed my voice, and kept my charge, my commandments, my statutes, and my laws."[81] The LORD does not make an explicit promise of protection to Isaac. However, there is a clear promise of protection implied when He tells Isaac that He "will be with [him]."

---

[79] Gen. 26:1–3
[80] In Genesis chapter 17, the LORD changes Abram's and Sarai's names to Abraham and Sarah.
[81] Gen. 26:4–5

The Promise of Protection to Jacob

Also, the "LORD God" tells Jacob, "I *am* the LORD God of Abraham thy father, and the God of Isaac: the land whereon thou liest, to thee will I give it, and to thy seed; And thy seed shall be as the dust of the earth, and thou shalt spread abroad to the west, and to the east, and to the north, and to the south: and in thee and in thy seed shall all the families of the earth be blessed. And, behold, I *am* with thee, and will keep thee in all places whither thou goest, and will bring thee again into this land; for I will not leave thee, until I have done *that* which I have spoken to thee of."[82]

The Promise of Protection to All Disciples

As with Abraham, Isaac, and Jacob, Jesus promises protection to His Apostles in Mathew 28:19–20.[83] Matthew 28:19–20 is commonly referred to as the "Great Commission." The Scripture reads, "Go ye therefore, and teach all nations, baptizing them in the name of the Father, and of the Son, and of the Holy Ghost: Teaching them to observe all things whatsoever I have commanded you: and, lo, I am with you alway, even unto the end of the world."

Hence, Jesus tells the Apostles that in the performance of the "Great Commission," He will be

---

82 Gen. 28:13–15
83 Matt. 28:16

with them. This is the same promise of protection that the LORD makes to Isaac and to Jacob. And though Jesus gives the "Great Commission" to His Apostles, I believe that the "Great Commission" and the accompanying promise of protection apply to all His "Holy Ghost-Filled" disciples. This includes those that will receive the Holy Spirit on the "Day of Pentecost,"[84] His disciples today, and His future disciples.

Tempting the LORD

As Christians, we should carry ourselves as true "ambassadors for Christ"[85] to have His assurance of protection. Jesus' promise of protection is like an insurance policy. Our protection is assured if we operate within the policy's constraints. If we operate outside the constraints of the policy, this protection is not assured. Thus, we must obey the commandment not to "tempt the Lord thy God,"[86] and heed Paul's warning to "neither let us tempt Christ, as some of them also tempted, and were destroyed of serpents."[87] We cannot behave in a way that would abuse His promise of protection. He gave us His Holy Spirit, love, and a sound mind

---

84 Acts 2:1–41
85 2 Cor. 5:20
86 Matt. 4:7
87 1 Cor. 10:9

to guide us in performing His mission and in conducting our daily lives.[88]

Jesus Does Not Tempt His Father
Satan tries to persuade Jesus to tempt His Father. Satan "saith unto him, If thou be the Son of God, cast thyself down: for it is written, He shall give his angels charge concerning thee: and in their hands they shall bear thee up, lest at any time thou dash thy foot against a stone. Jesus said unto him, It is written again, Thou shalt not tempt the Lord thy God."[89] Jesus makes clear that throwing Himself down to show that His Father will send His angels to catch Him will be tempting His Father and abusing His shield of protection.

Another time when Jesus avoids tempting His Father occurs when the chief priests and the Pharisees gather to decide what they should do with Jesus.[90] "Caiaphas, being the high priest that same year, said unto them, Ye know nothing at all, Nor consider that it is expedient for us, that one man should die for the people, and that the whole nation perish not. And this spake he not of himself: but being high priest that year, he prophesied that Jesus should die for that nation; And not for

---

88 2 Tim. 1:7; Jhn. 14:16, 26; 15:26; 16:7
89 Matt. 4:6–7
90   Jhn. 11:47–48

that nation only, but that also he should gather together in one the children of God that were scattered abroad. Then from that day forth they took counsel together for to put him to death."[91]

Jesus neither responds to the threats by flaunting His protection from His Father nor does Jesus responds in fear. Instead, Jesus "walked no more openly among the Jews; but went thence unto a country near to the wilderness, into a city called Ephraim, and there continued with his disciples."[92]

Joseph Does Not Tempt the LORD
When the "the angel of the Lord appeareth to Joseph in a dream, saying, Arise, and take the young child and his mother, and flee into Egypt, and be thou there until I bring thee word: for Herod will seek the young child to destroy him,"[93] Joseph does not say, "No, I will stay because the LORD will protect us from Herod." Instead, Joseph "arose, he took the young child and his mother by night, and departed into Egypt: And was there until the death of Herod: that it might be fulfilled which was spoken of the Lord by the prophet, saying, Out of Egypt have I called my son."[94]

---

91 Jhn. 11:49–53
92 Jhn. 11:54
93 Matt. 2:13
94 Matt. 2:14–15

David Does Not Tempt the LORD

When Saul "sent messengers unto David's house, to watch him, and to slay him in the morning: and Michal David's wife told him, saying, If thou save not thy life to night, to morrow thou shalt be slain."[95] We note that David does not say, "No, I will stay because the LORD will protect me." Instead, "Michal let David down through a window: and [David] went, and fled, and escaped."[96]

Moreover, when "there came a messenger to David, saying, The hearts of the men of Israel are after Absalom."[97] David does not say he will stay because the LORD will provide him protection. Instead, "David said unto all his servants that were with him at Jerusalem, Arise, and let us flee; for we shall not else escape from Absalom: make speed to depart, lest he overtake us suddenly, and bring evil upon us, and smite the city with the edge of the sword. And the king's servants said unto the king, Behold, thy servants are ready to do whatsoever my lord the king shall appoint. And the king went forth, and all his household after him. And the king left ten women, which were concubines, to keep the house. And the king went

---

95 1 Sam. 19:11
96 1 Sam. 19:12
97 2 Sam. 15:13

forth, and all the people after him, and tarried in a place that was far off."[98]

These are only a few examples of when Jesus, Joseph, and David did not tempt the Father. There are also examples of not tempting the LORD when the threat comes from diseases like leprosy and diseases that may come from touching dead bodies. The LORD can, and He has healed people of these diseases.[99] However, just as with Jesus, Joseph, and David, the LORD requires us to use the Holy Spirit, love, and the sound mind He gives us to take all the precautions He provides. The LORD instructs His people to avoid contact, to perform specific procedures after coming in contact, and to quarantine themselves to avoid coming in contact with others.[100] Moreover, people cannot unquarantined themselves; they are to seek the Priests for the official proclamation of when their quarantine is over.[101]

---

98 2 Sam. 15:14–17
99 2 Kin. 5:1–14, Matt. 8:1–3, Luk. 17:11–19
100 Lev. 13–14, Num. 19
101 Matt. 8:3–4, Lev. 13–14

CHAPTER 8

The "Lord GOD" in Genesis 15:2

The first clause of Genesis 15:2 reads, "And Abram said, Lord GOD, what wilt thou give me." The word "GOD" is in all capital letters and the word "Lord" is not. When we see this pattern in the KJV, we know that the Hebrew "יְהֹוִה" (yeh-ho-vee') is being translated, and it means "Jehovah"—used primarily in the combination 'Lord Jehovah'."[102] Thus, Abram knows this Person in the Trinity by His name, "JEHOVAH," and he addresses Him by His Name. This is the "JEHOVAH God," Jesus, that is in Genesis chapters 2 and 3.

---

102 Brown-Driver-Briggs, H3069

CHAPTER 9

"Covenant of Promise" Anxieties

Just as we should not tempt God, we should also understand that our anxieties do not represent a lack of faith or the tempting of God. Genesis 15:2–3 reads, "And Abram said, Lord GOD, what wilt thou give me, seeing I go childless, and the steward of my house is this Eliezer of Damascus? And Abram said, Behold, to me thou hast given no seed: and, lo, one born in my house is mine heir."[103] The anxiety that Abram expresses is due to him not understanding "how" and "when" the LORD will: (1) make of him a great nation, (2) bless him, (3) make his name great, (4) make him a blessing, (5) bless them that bless him, (6) curse them that curse him, and (7) in him shall all families of the earth be blessed. This set of promises forms the

---

103 Gen. 15:2–3

"Covenant of Promise." Abram's faith and obedience to God's commands are what is most important, not Abram's anxieties.

The Response to Abram's Anxieties

In Genesis 15:4–6, The LORD shows that He understands Abram's anxiety about being childless, and He addresses them by saying, "This shall not be thine heir; but he that shall come forth out of thine own bowels shall be thine heir. And he brought him forth abroad, and said, Look now toward heaven, and tell the stars, if thou be able to number them: and he said unto him, So shall thy seed be. And he believed in the LORD; and he counted it to him for righteousness."[104]

The LORD confirms His promises, provides more details, and He gives Abram a vision of his future descendants that cannot be numbered. (The significance of Abram's "seed" being uncountable will be discussed later in chapter 18.) Reiterating His promises, providing more details, and providing a vision of the future were all that the LORD could do because the "Covenant of Promise" is based on the Word of the LORD and the word of Abram.

---

104 Gen. 15:4–6

The Two Stipulations

The LORD gives Abram two broad stipulations concerning the "Covenant of Promise": He must believe the Word of the LORD, and he must dwell with the LORD and his seed in an exclusive manner. Thus, the two broad stipulations are faith and exclusivity. The faith stipulation is unspoken, but it is an inherent requirement of the "Covenant of Promise." This is because "without faith it is impossible to please [God],"[105] and Abram's obedience is evidence of his faith.

The Faith Stipulation

By Genesis chapter 15, Abram is 78 years old,[106] Sarai is 68 years old,[107] and they are childless. Moreover, Abram has completed his part of the covenant and is waiting on the LORD. Abram believes the LORD's promises, but he lacks an understanding of "how" and "when" the LORD will make his descendants as uncountable as the stars and give his descendants a land that is already inhabited.[108]

---

[105] Heb. 11:6
[106] Jasher 16:20–22
[107] Sarah, according to Gen. 17:17, was ten years younger than Abraham.
[108] Gen. 12:7

Abram demonstrates faith through his obedience. Yet, he shows his lack of understanding by offering up "Eliezer of Damascus" to be his heir. Thus, faith is not the lack of anxiety in performing God's mission—anxiety is a natural part of the human nature that God gave us. Faith is the demonstration of obedience and perseverance despite our anxieties, and our obedience and perseverance are evidence of our faith.[109]

The Threefold Path of Abram's Faith: Abram demonstrates his faith in three ways. First, Abram diligently and sincerely seeks to know and to understand the LORD, His will, and "what" He has promised him. Abram uses his relationship with the LORD to communicate with Him to gain this knowledge and understanding. The LORD appears to Abram in the flesh, in visions, and speaks to him directly.

For us today, the LORD does not appear in the flesh. And in general, the LORD does not appear to us in visions or speak to us directly to address our specific concerns as He did with Abram. Instead, Jesus said that He would "not leave [us] comfortless."[110] Jesus prays "to the Father, and

---

109 This is a rewording of Heb. 11:1.
110 Jhn. 14:18

he . . . [gave us] another Comforter, that he may abide with [us] for ever."[111]

Thus, just as Jesus is a "Comforter" to His disciples, the "Holy Ghost, whom the Father will send in [His] name, he shall teach [us] all things, and bring all things to [our] remembrance, whatsoever I have said unto you."[112] This "Holy Ghost" dwells within us and gives us power and comfort to be effective witnesses for Jesus.[113] We must use the Holy Spirit, love, and the sound mind that the LORD gives us to study, to know, and to understand His Holy Word.

Second, after gaining knowledge and understanding of the LORD's Will and promises, Abram believes the LORD. He believes while not understanding "how" the LORD will protect him and "how" and "when" the LORD will fulfill His promises. Because Abram believes, "the LORD counted it to him for righteousness."[114] Thus, we cannot just know and understand the LORD's Word; we must believe the LORD's Word.

---

111 Jhn. 14:16
112 Jhn. 14:26
113 Acts 1:8, Luk. 1:35, Rom. 15:19
114 Gen. 15:6

Lastly, Abram aligns his words and actions to the LORD's promises. In Genesis chapter 12, we read that "Abram departed, as the LORD directed; and Lot went with him: and Abram was seventy and five years old when he departed out of Haran."[115] However, the LORD first calls Abram "when he was in Mesopotamia, before he dwelt in [Harran]."[116] Thus, he departs from there first.

Additionally, Abram keeps his promise to "not take from [the inhabitants of the land] a thread even to a shoelatchet, and that [he] will not take any thing that is thine."[117] Thus, believing, overcoming anxieties, and seeking knowledge and understanding of the LORD, His Will, His Word, and His promises are not enough. We must align our words and actions with His Word, Will, and His Promises.

The overcoming of anxieties and the seeking of knowledge and understanding are characteristics of Abram and other great men of God, like Moses, Elijah, and John the Baptist. These men demonstrated evidence of their faith through their obedience and perseverance. Yet, they had anxieties.

---

115 Gen. 12:4
116 Acts 7:2
117 Gen. 14:23

Moses' Anxieties: After speaking to Moses through the burning bush, but before Moses "took his wife and his sons, and set them upon an ass, and he returned to the land of Egypt,"[118] God addresses Moses' anxieties about returning to Egypt by refocusing him away from his fears and more toward the power that He will give him, the love that he has for his brethren in Egypt, and his sound mind to understand and to follow His plan.

God does not want us to base our decisions and actions on fear and anxiety. "For God hath not given us the spirit of fear; but of power, and of love, and of a sound mind."[119] God wants us to rely upon the power of His Holy Spirit, the love for the brethren that He commands us to have, and the sound mind that He gives us to understand His Word, His Instruction, and to grow in godly Wisdom.

Elijah's Anxieties: In 1 Kings chapter 19, Elijah flees after hearing that Jezebel wants to kill him.[120] He tells the LORD, "It is enough; now, O LORD, take away my life; for I am not better than my fathers."[121] The LORD does not express dis-

---

118 Exo. 4:20
119 2 Tim. 1:7
120 1 Kin. 19:1–4
121 1 Kin. 19:4

appointment in Elijah; He comforts and reassures him. While Elijah lay asleep "under a juniper tree, behold, then an angel touched him, and said unto him, Arise and eat. And he looked, and, behold, there was a cake baken on the coals, and a cruse of water at his head. And he did eat and drink, and laid him down again."[122]

Later, the LORD asks Elijah, "What doest thou here, Elijah?"[123] Elijah replies, "I have been very jealous for the LORD God of hosts: for the children of Israel have forsaken thy covenant, thrown down thine altars, and slain thy prophets with the sword; and I, even I only, am left; and they seek my life, to take it away."[124]

The LORD listens to Elijah and addresses his anxieties by telling him "to return on thy way to the wilderness of Damascus: and when thou comest, anoint Hazael to be king over Syria: And Jehu the son of Nimshi shalt thou anoint to be king over Israel: and Elisha the son of Shaphat of Abelmeholah shalt thou anoint to be prophet in thy room. And it shall come to pass, that him that escapeth the sword of Hazael shall Jehu slay: and him that escapeth from the sword of Jehu shall

---

122 1 Kin. 19:5, 6
123 1 Kin. 19:9
124 1 Kin. 19:10

Elisha slay. Yet I have left me seven thousand in Israel, all the knees which have not bowed unto Baal, and every mouth which hath not kissed him."[125]

Thus, the LORD tells Elijah that He has a few more tasks for him before He takes him, that He wants him to know that he is far from being alone, and that He wants him to train up his successor. We all, at times, find ourselves, like Elijah, feeling alone and anxious. And, even with his feelings of anxiety and loneliness, Elijah went on to do what the LORD asked him to do.

Furthermore, we must take note that one of the tasks for Elijah is to train up and anoint his replacement. This is a critical task for all leaders to observe. It is not until after Elijah has trained up and anointed Elisha that the LORD allows Elijah to pass the mantle to Elisha and be called to rest in the Second Book of Kings.[126]

John the Baptist's Anxieties: John the Baptist shows anxiety about Jesus being the Messiah. When John the Baptist is in prison facing a death sentence, he hears "the works of Christ, he sent

---

125 1 Kin. 19:15–18
126 2 Kin. 2:11–14

two of his disciples, And said unto him, Art thou he that should come, or do we look for another?"[127]

Jesus does not scold John the Baptist for his anxiety. Instead, "Jesus answered and said unto them, Go and shew John again those things which ye do hear and see: The blind receive their sight, and the lame walk, the lepers are cleansed, and the deaf hear, the dead are raised up, and the poor have the gospel preached to them. And blessed is he, whosoever shall not be offended in me."[128] Jesus also declares, "Among them that are born of women there hath not risen a greater than John the Baptist: notwithstanding he that is least in the kingdom of heaven is greater than he."[129]

Let God Help Us Overcome Our Anxieties: The LORD understands our anxieties, and He provides us reassurance and understanding in His Holy Word. We must realize that courage is not doing the right thing in the absence of fear. "Courage is not the absence of fear, but rather the assessment that something else is more important than fear."[130]

---

[127] Matt. 11:2–3
[128] Matt. 11:4–6
[129] Matt. 11:11
[130] Brunner, Jeryl. "On the Anniversary of FDR's Birth, Read His 15 Greatest Quotes." Parade. Parade: Entertainment, Recipes, Health, Life, Holidays, January 30, 2015. https://

Those great men exercised the measure of faith that the LORD gave them to overcome their fears of embarrassment, inadequacy, rejection, etc., and boldly did the things that the LORD told them. Their boldness was sincere and came from praying, being led by the Holy Spirit, and from being tested in their faith, knowledge, and understanding of the LORD. These great men's faith, in the end, is far greater than the faith that they had in the beginning.

Faith, like a muscle, must be exercised. The LORD gives us all a measure of faith,[131] but the size and strength of our faith depend, in general, on how much we exercise our faith. These men used their sound minds, love, and the power of the Holy Spirit to exercise and strengthen their faith to the point that they risked their lives to do the will of the LORD.

Furthermore, when we, like Abram, Moses, Elijah, and John the Baptist, reach points in our lives when we do not understand what the LORD is doing, or we read Scriptures that we do not understand, we should realize that asking for understanding is not

---

parade.com/370879/jerylbrunner/on-the-anniversary-of-fdrs-birth-read-his-15-greatest-quotes/#:~:text=%E2%80%9CCourage%20is%20not%20the%20absence,be%20our%20doubts%20of%20to-day.%E2%80%9D. Retrieved on 18 2022April.

131 Rom. 12:3

wrong. What we see in Abram is a man of strong faith, in a difficult situation, seeking knowledge and understanding from the LORD to help him move forward in doing the LORD's will. We should do the same.

The Exclusivity Stipulation
Abram's desire to keep his part of the "Covenant of Promise," which includes the exclusivity stipulation, is demonstrated when "the king of Sodom said unto Abram, Give me the persons, and take the goods to thyself,"[132] Abram tells the king of Sodom, "I have lift up mine hand unto the LORD, the most high God, the possessor of heaven and earth, That I will not take from a thread even to a shoelatchet, and that I will not take any thing that is thine, lest thou shouldest say, I have made Abram rich: Save only that which the young men have eaten, and the portion of the men which went with me, Aner, Eshcol, and Mamre; let them take their portion."[133] Abram promises to dwell with his descendants and the LORD under the "Covenant of Promise," exclusively, in the "Promised Land." The "Promised Land" is a carnal kingdom on earth that points to a spiritual kingdom in Heaven.

---

132 Gen. 14:21
133 Gen. 14:22–24

The Exclusivity Stipulation and Love: Jesus gives us a new commandment: "That [we] love one another; as [He] have loved [us], that ye also love one another. By this shall all men know that ye are my disciples, if ye have love one to another."[134] He also confirmed an old commandment that He gave Abram that we have a sincere desire to dwell with Jesus and with our spiritual brethren, exclusively, in a spiritual kingdom on earth and in Heaven. Jesus speaks of this spiritual kingdom in Heaven when He said, "In my Father's house are many mansions: if it were not so, I would have told you. I go to prepare a place for you. And if I go and prepare a place for you, I will come again, and receive you unto myself; that where I am, there ye may be also."[135]

We cannot start meeting the requirements for dwelling in Heaven after entering Heaven. We must be already meeting the requirements before entering Heaven. Otherwise, we will not make it to Heaven. We must appreciate just how "good and how pleasant it is for brethren to dwell together in unity!"[136]

---

134 Jhn. 13:34, 35
135 Jhn. 14:2–3
136 Psa. 133:1

Loved Ones and the "Great Commission": We must share the Word of God with our spouses, family members, friends, and others while we are alive. Jesus tells us to, "Go ye therefore, and teach all nations, baptizing them in the name of the Father, and of the Son, and of the Holy Ghost: Teaching them to observe all things whatsoever I have commanded you: and, lo, I am with you alway, even unto the end of the world."[137] We must share the Word of God while we are alive. This is because once we die, or potential converts die, there is nothing more we can do.[138] However, if they die in Christ, we have hope of seeing them again.

When "the LORD struck the child that Uriah's wife bare unto David, and it was very sick. David therefore besought God for the child; and David fasted, and went in, and lay all night upon the earth. And the elders of his house arose, and went to him, to raise him up from the earth: but he would not, neither did he eat bread with them. And it came to pass on the seventh day, that the child died. But when David perceived that the child was dead: therefore David said unto his servants, Is the child dead? And they said, He is dead. Then David arose from the earth, and washed, and anointed

---

137 Matt. 28:19, 20
138 Ecc. 9:10

himself, and changed his apparel, and came into the house of the LORD, and worshipped: then he came to his own house; and when he required, they set bread before him, and he did eat."[139]

David's conduct after the child's death marvels his servants. They asked him, "What thing is this that thou hast done? Thou didst fast and weep for the child, while it was alive; but when the child was dead, thou didst rise and eat bread."[140] David responds by saying, "While the child was yet alive, I fasted and wept: for I said, Who can tell whether GOD will be gracious to me, that the child may live? But now he is dead, wherefore should I fast? Can I bring him back again? I shall go to him, but he shall not return to me."[141]

So, what is the point? We must "go out into the highways and hedges, and compel them to come in, that [His] house may be filled,"[142] "while it is day: the night cometh, when no man can work."[143] In David's case, he has hope of seeing the child again. But, in the case of a person unsaved in Christ, once death comes and they die in their sins, there is no hope of seeing them again. The

---

139 2 Sam. 12:15–20
140 2 Sam. 12: 21
141 2 Sam. 12:22–23
142 Luk. 14:23
143 Jhn. 9:4

unsaved only have hope while they are alive. This is because eternal life is not based on how we once lived our lives. Eternal life is based on how we are living our lives in Christ when we die.

So, without pushing people away, we must take every opportunity to ensure that our spouses, family members, friends, and others have ample chances to choose Christ, regardless of how they lived or are currently living their lives. For like David, if we ever want to see them again, we must give them ample opportunities to accept Jesus as their Lord and Savior. This is because Heaven is an exclusive community. Only the children of God are allowed to dwell there. The wicked and those that do not accept Jesus as their Lord and Savior are not allowed to dwell in Heaven.

Discerning Wicked People from Other People: The LORD wants Abram's "Covenant of Promise" descendants to separate themselves from their surrounding inhabitants. Paul explains to the church at Corinth how this applies to them. He states that he wrote "in an epistle not to company with fornicators: Yet not altogether with the fornicators of this world, or with the covetous, or extortioners, or with idolaters; for then must ye needs go out of the world."[144] Paul explains that

---

[144] 1 Cor. 5:9–10

you must have some association with these types of people because you dwell in this world.

Nevertheless, Paul cautions them that they should not "keep company, if any man that is called a brother be a fornicator, or covetous, or an idolater, or a railer, or a drunkard, or an extortioner; with such an one no not to eat. For what have I to do to judge them also that are without? do not ye judge them that are within? But them that are without God judgeth. Therefore put away from among yourselves that wicked person."[145]

Paul instructs the church at Corinth to "put away from among [themselves] that wicked person."[146] Thus, we must be able to distinguish between wicked people, people caught in a fault, and people we may consider enemies. This is because we are instructed that "if a man be overtaken in a fault, [we] which are spiritual, restore such an one in the spirit of meekness; considering thyself, lest thou also be tempted,"[147] and we are instructed to "bear ye one another's burdens, and so fulfil the law of Christ."[148]

---

145 1 Cor. 5:11–13
146 1 Cor. 5:13
147 Gal. 6:1
148 Gal. 6:2

Moreover, Jesus instructs us: "Love [our] enemies, bless them that curse you, do good to them that hate you, and pray for them which despitefully use you, and persecute you; That ye may be the children of your Father which is in heaven: for he maketh his sun to rise on the evil and on the good, and sendeth rain on the just and on the unjust. For if ye love them which love you, what reward have ye? do not even the publicans the same?"[149] Therefore, we must treat people caught in a fault and our enemies differently from wicked people.

We "all have sinned, and come short of the glory of God."[150] Consequently, the fact that a person has sinned cannot be a distinguishing factor between a sinner and an evil person. Likewise, we cannot say that our enemies are evil people. In general, an "enemy" is a person that we have enmity toward based on something personal: jealousy, envy, misunderstandings, or for various other reasons. Our enemies may, or may not, be evil. In the same way, our enemies should not consider us as evil.

Conversely, "evil people" are sinners with evil intent that is not based on personal enmity. Their evil intent is solely based on their own self-serving

---

149 Matt. 5:44–46
150 Rom. 3:23

desires. Evil people do not have to know you, or have a personal relationship with you, to have ill intentions toward you. In fact, just having a personal relationship with evil people could be a threat to your life, health, and livelihood, and to the life, health, and livelihood of your family and friends. Therefore, the Bible warns us to not "desire to be with [evil people,][151] and to "have no fellowship with the unfruitful works of darkness, but rather reprove them."[152]

For example, evil people, such as serial killers, do not have to know you to kill you, scammers to scam you, or psychopaths to manipulate you and destroy your reputation and your relationships with your family, friends, employer, and church. We must diligently seek to avoid these people. A relationship, for example, with people like Jeffrey Dahmer, Jeffrey Epstein, and Ted Bundy puts you in a position to potentially become their next victim, or to accompany them in their inevitable downfall. These people seek to take your life, destroy your life, increase their wealth, and achieve a depraved personal pleasure.

Evil people are the pimps that establish relationships with young girls and boys to have them as a

---

151 Pro. 24:1
152 Eph. 5:11

source of income as prostitutes. They are the drug dealers that establish relationships with people to lead them to become dependent customers. They are also the ambitious psychopaths that deceitfully establish and use relationships with coworkers and fellow church members to acquire money, position, and power.

Evil people are beyond our help; even God gave some over to a reprobate mind.[153] We will know evil people in the same way we will know false prophets—by their fruits.[154] Evil people will tell us who they are in their words and actions, and we must believe them. Evil people may—or may not—be lost; only God knows.

We must not endanger ourselves, our families, and our friends trying to save evil people. The LORD is concerned about His Spiritual children falling victim to evil people. He is concerned about His Spiritual children adopting and propagating evil ways through any association they may have with evil people.

---

153 Rom. 1:28
154 Matt. 7:15–16

CHAPTER 10

Reconciling Genesis and Exodus

Verse 7 reads, "And he said unto him, I am the LORD that brought thee out of Ur of the Chaldees, to give thee this land to inherit it."[155] In this verse, a Person in the Trinity introduces Himself as "JEHOVAH." Yet, in Exodus 6:3, a Person in the Trinity says, "I appeared unto Abraham, unto Isaac, and unto Jacob, by *the name of* God Almighty, but by my name JEHOVAH was I not known to them."

The Person in Exodus 6:3 cannot be the same Person in Genesis 15:7 because "God is not a man, that he should lie; neither the son of man, that he should repent: hath he said, and shall he not do it? Or hath he spoken, and shall he not make

---

155 Gen. 15:7

it good?"[156] In this Scripture, "God the Father" says that neither He nor His Son, who He refers to as the "Son of Man," can lie. Thus, the Person in Genesis 15:7, the "Son of God," and the One in Exodus 6:3, "God the Father, are both in the Trinity, but they are different Persons that share the same name, JEHOVAH.

JEHOVAH Is God's Surname

Both "God the Father" and "God the Son" share the same surname, "JEHOVAH." We find this pattern of descendants sharing the surname of the father in OT Scripture. The Hebrew word translated "surname" in the KJV appears four times. This Hebrew word is "kânâh," and it is translated twice as "title"[157] in the Book of Job and twice as "surname" in the Book of Isaiah. In Isaiah 44:5 and Isaiah 45:4, this Hebrew word refers to Israel as a "surname."

Israel Is a Surname

God gives Israel a surname,[158] and his descendants are often referred to as "Israel."[159] In fact, determining if Scriptures refer to Israel "the man"

---

156 Num. 23:19
157 Job 32:21, 22
158 Gen. 32:28, Isa. 44:5
159 Deu. 4:1, 6:4; Jos. 8:14, 11:8; Jdg. 2:14, 3:10; 1 Sam. 2:32, 4:2

or Israel "his descendants" is a matter of context. Likewise, when it comes to "JEHOVAH," we must consider the context. When we read "JEHOVAH" in the Scriptures, context helps us to determine if the Scripture is referring to "God the Father" or "God the Son," Jesus.

Adam Is a Surname
The Hebrew word translated as Adam in the KJV is "אָדָם" ('âdâm).[160] This Hebrew word "אָדָם" is the surname for Adam, the man, and Adam's descendants, man/mankind.[161] Consequently, the only way to determine if "אָדָם" refers to Adam the man or man/mankind is to look at the context of the Scripture.

The KJV of Hosea 6:7 reads, "But they like men have transgressed the covenant." The KJV translates "אָדָם" as "men." However, the New International Version (NIV) translates "אָדָם" as "Adam," the American Standard Version (ASV) translates it as "Adam," and the New King James Version (NKJV) translates this Hebrew word as "men." Thus, the context is essential in determining if this Hebrew word should translate as

---

160 Strong's Concordance H121
161 Strong's Concordance H120 and H121 is the same Hebrew word.

Adam, the man, or as Adam's descendants, man/mankind.

The JEHOVAH Surname in Isaiah

Another OT Scripture that points to "God the Father" and "God the Son" sharing the same surname is Isaiah 44:6. In Isaiah 44:6, "God the Father" is referred to as the LORD (JEHOVAH), the King of Israel, and His Redeemer ("God the Son") is referred to as the LORD (JEHOVAH) of Hosts.[162] In this verse, both "God the Father" and "God the Son" are depicted as having the same surname, JEHOVAH. Jesus, "God the Son," is referred to in this verse as "God the Father's Redeemer." Jesus is not referred to as the King of Israel, "God the Father" is. This is consistent with an interpretation of Exodus 24:10 and John 20:28. In Exodus 24:10, Jesus is referred to as the "God of Israel,"[163] and, in John 20:28, Thomas calls Jesus "my God."

The JEHOVAH Surname in Jeremiah

In Jeremiah 23:5, we read that the LORD (JEHOVAH) "will raise unto David a righteous Branch, and a King shall reign and prosper, and shall execute judgment and justice in the earth."[164]

---

[162] Isa. 54:5, Jer. 50:34
[163] In Exo. 24:10, Jesus is referred to as the "God of Israel."
[164] Jer. 23:5

Moreover, we know from Jeremiah 23:6 that "his name whereby he shall be called, THE LORD (JEHOVAH) OUR RIGHTEOUSNESS."[165] Thus, JEHOVAH is the name of the Branch that is spoken of in Jeremiah 23:5, and the name of this Branch, as translated by the KJV of the NT, is Jesus. Thus, Jesus is the Branch, or JEHOVAH, in Jeremiah 23:5.

All Three Have the Surname JEHOVAH

The Great Commission: Matthew 28:19 reads, "Go ye therefore, and teach all nations, baptizing them in the name of the Father, and of the Son, and of the Holy Ghost." B. B. Warfield writes that this verse "does not say, 'In the names [plural] of the Father and of the Son and of the Holy Ghost'; nor yet (what might be taken to be equivalent to that), 'In the name of the Father, and in the name of the Son, and in the name of the Holy Ghost,' as if we had to deal with three separate Beings [with three different names]. Nor, on the other hand, does it say, 'In the name of the Father, Son and Holy Ghost,' as if 'the Father, Son and Holy Ghost' might be taken as merely three designations of a single person."[166]

---

165 Jer. 23:6
166 B.B. Warfield, "Trinity," from the International Standard Bible Encyclopedia (general editor James Orr), 1915, IV, 3017

Instead, B. B. Warfield writes that Matthew 28:19 "asserts the unity of the three by combining them all within the bounds of the single Name; and then throws up into emphasis the distinctness of each by introducing them in turn with the repeated article: 'In the name of the Father, and of the Son, and of the Holy Ghost.' "These three, the Father, and the Son, and the Holy Ghost, each stand in some clear sense over against the others in distinct personality: these three, the Father, and the Son, and the Holy Ghost, all unite in some profound sense in the common participation of the one Name."[167] Hence, all three share the same name, "JEHOVAH."

Baptizing in Jesus' Name Only in the Book of Acts: B. B. Warfield's interpretation of Matthew 28:19 explains why no one is baptized under the explicit "Great Commission" statement of "in the name of the Father, and of the Son, and of the Holy Ghost"[168] in the Book of Acts. For example, on the "Day of Pentecost," someone asks, "Men and brethren, what shall we do?"[169] Peter replies, "Repent, and be baptized every one of you in the name of Jesus (Jehoshua, JEHOVAH-saved) Christ

---

167 B.B. Warfield, "Trinity," 3017
168 Matt. 28:19
169 Acts 2:37

for the remission of sins, and ye shall receive the gift of the Holy Ghost."[170]

In Acts 2:38, Peter does not explicitly state the "Great Commission." Instead, Peter tells the people to be baptized in one name, "Jehoshua" (JEHOVAH-saved). Peter does not use Jesus' translated-English name; he uses Jesus' Hebrew name, "Jehoshua." And by instructing the crowd to be baptized in the name of "Jehoshua," he is telling them to be baptized in the name "of the Father, and of the Son, and of the Holy Ghost," which is "JEHOVAH"—because they all share the same name, JEHOVAH. Thus, in this case, the translation to English obscures the true meaning.

The Ephesians Surname Account: Another reference to JEHOVAH being a surname is in the Book of Ephesians. In Ephesians 3:13, Paul tells the Ephesians that he "desire that [they] faint not at [his] tribulations for [them], which is [their] glory." Paul adds, "For this cause I bow my knees unto the Father of our Lord Jesus Christ, Of whom the whole family in heaven and earth is named."[171] Paul states that the whole family of "God the Father" that is in heaven and in earth are given "God the Father's" surname, JEHOVAH.

---

170 Acts 2:38
171 Eph. 3:14–16

Moses, the Patriarchs, and God's Name

Moses

"God the Father" neither tells Moses that His name is "I AM THAT I AM" in Exodus 3:14, nor does He tell Moses that His name is "God Almighty" in Exodus 6:3. "God the Father" has only one name, "JEHOVAH." In Exodus 3:14, He tells Moses one of His attributes—a self-existent and always existing being that can meet all our needs. "God the Father" does not declare His name to Moses until the next verse. In Exodus 3:15, "God the Father" tells Moses that His name is "JEHOVAH."

In this verse, "God the Father" tells Moses to "say unto the children of Israel, The LORD God of your fathers, the God of Abraham, the God of Isaac, and the God of Jacob, hath sent me unto you: this is my name for ever, and this is my memorial unto all generations." "LORD" is how the KJV translates God's name, "JEHOVAH." Thus, "God the Father" tells Moses that His name is JEHOVAH. And, to be more precise, "God the Father" uses the term "LORD God." This means that "God the Father" tells Moses that He is the God named JEHOVAH.

The Patriarchs

In Exodus 6:3, the translators added the phrase "*the name of.*" We know this because it is in italics.[172] The original Scripture reads, "And I appeared unto Abraham, unto Isaac, and unto Jacob, by God Almighty, but by my name JEHOVAH was I not known to them." This means that this Person in the Trinity does not say that His name is "God Almighty"; "God Almighty" is a title, not a name. Instead, this Person of the Trinity, "God the Father," says that the Patriarchs: Abraham, Isaac, and Jacob, only knew Him by His title, "God Almighty." They did not know him by His name, "JEHOVAH." They, however, knew "God the Son" by His surname JEHOVAH. But, they only knew "God the Father" by His titles: "Elohim" and "God Almighty." "God the Father" first reveals His name to man at the burning bush in Exodus 3:15, and it was to Moses.

The Son Is Separate but Equal to the Father

Jesus not only shares His Father's name; He shares His Father's kind and form. Jesus, "being in the form of God, thought it not robbery to be equal with God."[173] This is what the Jews respond to when Jesus said, "My Father worketh hitherto, and I work."[174] They "sought the more to kill him,

---

172 James Melton Publications. The italicized words in the King James Bible. Accessed April 24, 2022. https://www.bible-believers.com/jmelton/italics.html.
173 Php. 2:6
174 Jhn. 5:17

because he not only had broken the sabbath, but said also that God was his Father, making himself equal with God."[175]

The Jews in John 5:18 do not accuse Jesus of claiming to be "God the Father," they accuse Him of claiming to be the "Son of God," and, thereby, claiming to be equal to "God the Father." Nowhere in the Bible is Jesus recorded claiming to be "God the Father." Jesus is consistently recorded in the Bible saying that He is the "Son of God."[176] And as the "Son of God," Jesus is equal in kind and form to "God the Father."

This logically follows the language in John 1:1–2 and in the previous discourse about Genesis chapters 1–3, John 1:3, and Colossians 1:16. In John 1:1–2, we read, "In the beginning was the Word, and the Word was with God, and the Word was God. He was in the beginning with God." These verses confirm that Jesus is before all creation and is with "God the Father" in the beginning. Moreover, since Jesus is the "Only Begotten Son"[177] of "God the Father," He is of the same kind and form as "God the Father."

---

175 Jhn. 5:18
176 Matt. 7:21, 10:32, 12:50; Luk. 2:49, 10:22, 22:42
177 Jhn. 3:16

Furthermore, a closer look at the Greek word translated as "God" in John 1:1–2 will make the previous points clearer. The KJV translates the Greek word "θεός" (theos) as "God" in John 1:1–2. This Greek word means "a deity, especially (with G3588) the supreme Divinity; figuratively a magistrate; by Hebraism very: - X exceeding, God, god [-ly, -ward]."[178] Thus, this Greek word refers to a being that is greater than man, or it may be a title. It does not refer to the name of a specific god. This Greek word corresponds to the Hebrew word "Elohim."

Therefore, if these two verses are read using the phrase "a deity," as defined in the Strong's Concordance, instead of the word "God," these verses will make more sense. They will then read, "In the beginning was the Word, and the Word was with [a deity], and the Word was [a deity]. He was in the beginning with [a deity]." And, since we know that the "Word" is Jesus, John is saying in John 1:1–2 that Jesus was with a deity, this deity is His Father, and He is a deity, just like His Father.

Moreover, the Greek word "θεός" (theos) is also used in Hebrews 1:8–9. If we make a similar replacement of "a deity/deity" in Hebrews 1:8–9,

---

178 Strong's Concordance, G2316

these verses will also be clearer. For example, these verses currently read, "But unto the Son he saith, Thy throne, O God, is for ever and ever: a sceptre of righteousness is the sceptre of thy kingdom. Thou hast loved righteousness, and hated iniquity; therefore God, even thy God, hath anointed thee with the oil of gladness above thy fellows."[179] These Scriptures refer to Jesus and "God the Father" as God, and the Greek word translated as "God" is "θεός" (theos).

If we replace "God" with "deity," these verses will read, "But unto the Son he saith, Thy throne, O **Deity**, is for ever and ever: a sceptre of righteousness is the sceptre of thy kingdom. Thou hast loved righteousness, and hated iniquity; therefore **Deity**, even thy **Deity**, hath anointed thee with the oil of gladness above thy fellows." Thus, these Scriptures make clear that Jesus and "God the Father" are Deities, that Jesus is subordinate to "God the Father," and that "God the Father" anointed Jesus "with the oil of gladness above thy fellows."

John 1:1–2 and Hebrews 1:7–9 do not say that Jesus is "God the Father." These verses make clear that Jesus is not a man. Jesus is a deity, like His Father. Jesus takes on the form of a man many

---

[179] Heb. 1:8–9

times in the Bible, but He is ultimately a deity like His Father. This is because the Spirit conceived in Him by the Holy Spirit[180] is the Spirit of a deity, His Spirit. However, His body was made from the dust of the ground, like a man.[181] This combination makes Jesus a living soul with a Spirit of a deity and a man's body.

The concept that the "Son of God," Jesus, is equal in kind and form to "God the Father" originates in Genesis chapter 1. This chapter reads that every plant and animal is designed to reproduce after its kind.[182] Eve is after the same kind and form as Adam, as we are after the same kind and form as our parents. As such, Jesus, as "[God the Father's] only begotten Son," must also be of the same kind and form as "God the Father."

Adam references this concept when he says that Eve "is now bone of my bones, and flesh of my flesh: she shall be called Woman, because she was taken out of Man."[183] Therefore, Eve is not Adam, but she is equal to, complementary, and the same kind and form as Adam. Eve is not a cow, she is

---

180 Matt. 1:20
181 Gen. 2:7
182 Gen. 1:11, 21, 24–25
183 Gen. 2:23

not a horse, she is not a deity, she is in the same form as Adam, a human being.

The "LORD God" forms and creates Eve to be a separate person that is equal to and of the same kind and form as Adam. He does this because "it is not good that the man should be alone; [He made] him an help meet for [Adam],"[184] and before then, "There was not found an help meet for him."[185] The animals are not of the same kind and form as Adam, and they are not equal to him like Eve.

---

184 Gen. 2:18
185 Gen. 2:20

CHAPTER 11

The Promised Land

Verse 8 reads, "And he said, Lord GOD, whereby shall I know that I shall inherit it?"[186] The "it" that Abram refers to is the land that he is currently in and the land that the LORD promised to give to his descendants, the "Promised Land." Abram is in the "Promised Land," but the LORD has not given him, or his descendants, possession of the "Land."

The "Promised Land" Comes First

The "Promised Land" and the exclusivity requirement came first. The "Promised Land" is a requirement and a token of dwelling in support of the set of promises involving Abram's seed. The LORD wants Abram's descendants to be separate from

---

186 Gen. 15:8

their surrounding inhabitants. This is to keep the inhabitants from teaching Abram's descendants "all their abominations, which they have done unto their gods; so should ye sin against the LORD your God."[187]

The "Promised Land" and "Rights of Sonship"

Requirements for Sonship

The LORD will use Abram's descendants to build for Himself "a kingdom of priests, and an holy nation"[188] that will dwell in the "Promised Land" with Him. No other people can dwell with the LORD in the "Promise Land." Only Abram's descendants with "rights of sonship." However, "rights of sonship" are not limited to only blood descendants of Abram. Several of Abram's descendants did not receive "rights of sonship."

For example, Ishmael and his descendants did not receive "rights of sonship,"[189] the descendants that Abraham had with Keturah and their descendants did not receive "rights of sonship,"[190] and Esau and his descendants did not receive "rights of sonship."[191] "Rights of sonship" are based on

---

187 Deu. 20:18
188 Exo.19:6
189 Gen. 25:5, 6
190 Gen. 25:1–6
191 Mal. 1:2, 3

spiritual blood, not physical blood, and they extend to "graffed in" strangers too.[192]

The requirements for "rights of sonship" were based on accepting the LORD as your God, the keeping of His commandments; the bearing of the token, or sign, of covenant membership; and, the keeping of the ordinances of four covenants: The "Covenant of Redemption," the "Noahic Covenant," the "Covenant of Promise," and the "Old Covenant." These four covenants were in effect until Jesus' death on the cross. The "Adamic Covenant" is no longer in effect. It was replaced by the "Covenant of Redemption."

There are tokens and ordinances associated with each of these four covenants, and they are consolidated with each successive covenant. In other words, the subsequent covenants do not make void the preceding covenants.[193] Thus, to maintain "rights of sonship," a member must adhere to all tokens and ordinances of four covenants. The only one that does not require an action by man is the "Noahic Covenant." This is because the token or ordinance of this Covenant is the rainbow,[194] and all that it requires is to dwell on the earth.

---

192 Rom. 11:11–24
193 Gal. 3:17
194 Gen. 9:1–17

The first of the four covenants that require active participation by man is the "Covenant of Redemption"; and, its token or ordinance is the substitutional sacrifice of a male lamb without spot or blemish. The next covenant is the "Covenant of Promise." Its token, or ordinance, is circumcision plus the token or ordinance for the "Covenant of Redemption." The next covenant is the "Old Covenant," and its token, or ordinance, includes daily and monthly sacrifices, the Sabbaths, the LORD's "Appointed Days," and the tokens, or ordinances, of the previous two: the "Covenant of Redemption" and the "Covenant of Promise."

The "Appointed Days" include the "Passover," the "Feast of Unleavened Bread," the "Feast of Firstfruits," the "Feast of Weeks," the "Feast of Trumpets," the "Day of Atonement," and the "Feast of Tabernacles." Furthermore, they require all circumcised males to sojourn in Jerusalem three times a year.[195]

Women, Not Members of the Covenants

Women are not members of the four aforementioned covenants. These covenants are exclusively male. The establishment of circumcision as a token of the "Covenant of Promise" is one requirement

---

[195] Exo. 23:14–17, Deu. 16:16

that prevents women from being members. Yet, women supported these covenants and benefited from the membership of their husbands, sons, fathers, and brothers. This changes with the "New Covenant." Under the "New Covenant," males and females receive the tokens of membership and participate in the ordinances: Water Baptism, Holy Ghost Baptism, Holy Communion,[196] and the Washing of the Saints' Feet.[197]

God Made Allowances for Strangers

The LORD always planned to bring in strangers.[198] He made allowances for them to have "rights of sonship" if they accept Him as their God and keep His laws. The LORD tells Moses, "When a stranger shall sojourn with thee, and will keep the Passover to the LORD, let all his males be circumcised, and then let him come near and keep it; and he shall be as one that is born in the land: for no uncircumcised person shall eat thereof. One law shall be to him that is homeborn, and unto the stranger that sojourneth among you."[199] Thus, sonship is not based on race, ethnicity, or having the physical blood of Abraham. Sonship is based

---

196 Luk. 22:14–20, Jhn. 13:1–20
197 Jhn. 13:1–15
198 Gal. 3:8
199 Exo. 12:48, 49

on a person's acceptance of the LORD as their God and on their obedience to Him.

The Casting Out of the "Promised Land"

The "Promised Land" serves the same purpose as the Garden of Eden and "New Jerusalem"—it is a dwelling place for the LORD's people on the Earth. The Garden of Eden was the carnal token of dwelling for the LORD's covenant with Adam. Likewise, "New Jerusalem" is the spiritual token of dwelling for Jesus' people in His spiritual "Church" on the Earth.

Like Adam and Eve, we are subject to being cast out when we break the covenant. We note that in the Book of Revelation, Satan and the angels that followed him are cast out of Heaven.[200] And, in the Books of 2 Kings and Jeremiah, we read that the Israelites are cast out of the "Promised Land."[201]

Token of Dwelling Ends with the Covenant

There is a difference in what happens to tokens of dwelling when a covenant is broken by an individual or individuals, and when a covenant is broken by the nation, or a people, for which the token of dwelling is established. For example,

---

200 Rev. 12:7–9
201 2 Kin. 17:6 , 25:8–21

when Satan and a third of the angels in Heaven rebel gainst God, they are cast out of Heaven,[202] but Heaven remains. Heaven is God's dwelling place, and it was not established for Satan or the angels. Thus, when Satan and a third of the angels rebelled against God, they broke an inherent covenant; when you dwell in someone else's home, you do not rebel or try to take over. The owner is likely to remove you from his home.

In contrast, when Adam breaks the covenant with "God the Father" and Jesus, Adam and Eve are both cast out of the Garden of Eden, and the Garden of Eden ceases to exist as an exclusive dwelling place for them and their descendants. The land is still somewhere on the earth, but it is no longer set aside by the LORD as an exclusive dwelling place for Adam and Eve and their descendants.

Likewise, the "Promised Land" was established as a dwelling place for the "Children of Israel" that are under the four previously mentioned covenants. Thus, when they, as the nation for which the token of dwelling is established, break the covenant, they are cast out of the "Promised Land." The Northern Kingdom of Israel is cast out in 722 BC. The Southern Kingdom of Judah is cast out in 588 BC.

---

202 Rev. 12:7–9

Once the "Children of Israel" are cast out, the "Promised Land" ceases to be the exclusive home for the people in the LORD's earthly kingdom. Neither is Jerusalem the earthly location where He symbolically dwells with His people. The land is still present. However, the land is no longer set aside by the LORD. Instead, the "Promised Land" degenerated into the spiritual version of the OT places named Sodom and Egypt by Paul's day.[203]

New Dwelling and Individual Tokens
Jesus fulfills and, thereby, ends the "Old Covenant," the "Covenants of Promise," and the "Covenant of Redemption" when He dies and rises from the grave. In doing so, He ends the covenants that gave the Israelites the authority to dwell in the "Promised Land" with the LORD. Moreover, the LORD replaces these covenants with the "New Covenant." He replaces the "Promised Land" and Jerusalem with the whole earth and the "New Jerusalem," respectively. The LORD replaces the Temple in Jerusalem with the bodies of His people under the "New Covenant."[204] He replaces physical circumcision of the flesh as an individual carnal token with the "Holy Ghost" as an individual spiritual token.[205] Lastly, the LORD replaces the

---

[203] Rev. 11:8, Isa. 1:9–10, Jer. 23:14, Eze. 16:44–46
[204] 1 Cor. 6:19–20
[205] Rom. 8:15–17, Acts 15:22–31

"Ark of the Covenant" for housing His law written in stone[206] with the heart of man for housing His spiritual law.

No longer is there a single-physical temple at a single-geographic location for "which the LORD your God shall choose to cause his name to dwell there; thither shall ye bring all that I command you; your burnt offerings, and your sacrifices, your tithes, and the heave offering of your hand, and all your choice vows which ye vow unto the LORD,"[207] like in the days of Solomon's Temple in Jerusalem.

No longer would the LORD require His men to travel to a single city on earth three times a year to worship Him. Moreover, the LORD would no longer require the men in His earthly Kingdom to be circumcised of the flesh. Instead, the LORD now gives His people on earth churches and dwellings throughout the earth for them to assemble themselves and to keep His new ordinances of Water Baptism, Holy Communion, and the Washing of the Saints' Feet.[208] Today, Jesus has a global-virtu-

---

206 Heb. 9:4
207 Deu. 12:11
208 Luk. 22:14–23, Jhn. 13:1–15, Matt. 28:16–20

al Jerusalem—the "New Jerusalem" in the Book of Revelation.[209]

The New Jerusalem

The "New Jerusalem" replaces the physical Jerusalem that the Romans destroyed in AD 70.[210] This new virtual, or spiritual, Jerusalem is connected by the same Holy Ghost that fell upon the Jews dwelling and sojourning in the physical Jerusalem on the "Day of Pentecost."[211] This is the "New Jerusalem, which cometh down out of heaven from my God."[212] It is "as towns without walls for the multitude of men and cattle therein."[213] For the LORD "will be unto her a wall of fire round about, and will be the glory in the midst of her."[214] The people in the "New Jerusalem" will bear Jesus and His Holy Ghost within their hearts and minds wherever they go.

The Holy Ghost is a gift from the LORD that is given based on the faith and the heart—the LORD

---

[209] Rev. 3: 12, 21:1–3, 24–27
[210] SCHAFER, PETER. "Pp 129-130." Essay. In History of the Jews in the Greco-Roman World;the Jews of Palestine from Alexander the Great to the Arab Conquest. ROUTLEDGE, 2003.
[211] Acts 2
[212] Rev. 3:12, 21:1–2
[213] Zec. 2:4
[214] Zec. 2:5

knows our faith and heart. Consequently, the LORD uses the Holy Ghost to identify the people that are in His "Church." And, thereby, they have a right to dwell in the "New Jerusalem." Thus, the Holy Ghost serves as a "wall of fire round about" the "New Jerusalem."

The Holy Ghost prevents people who are not of the LORD's "Church" from entering the "New Jerusalem." False Christians may fool man by deceitfully submitting to Water Baptism and confessing their faith, but true citizenship in the "New Jerusalem" is based on the indwelling of the Holy Ghost. And the indwelling of the Holy Ghost is based on the heart.

Moreover, the LORD sent His Holy Ghost as a token of His presence, as a token of the spiritual circumcision within each "New Covenant" member on earth, and as a type of "Kinsman Redeemer."[215] And, as a type of "Kinsman Redeemer," the Holy Ghost serves as a substitute husband and father for Jesus on earth. Thus, while Jesus reigns from Heaven, the Holy Ghost takes care of Jesus' widowed "Church," keeps Jesus' name alive, and He bears disciples, not in His name, but in Jesus' name.

---

[215] Gen 38:8–10, Deu. 25:5–10

Today, Believers, and future Believers, in Jesus exist in one of three states. The first state is as a carnal being, in a carnal body, and in a carnal world. The second state is in the Spiritual Wilderness, or the "New Jerusalem." In this second state, Believers are transitioning from being a carnal being to being a spiritual being. They are also in cohabitation with the Holy Ghost. Their bodies are "the temple of the Holy Ghost *which is* in [them], which ye have of God."[216]

Moreover, in the "New Jerusalem," Believers are being trained that "true worshippers shall worship the Father in spirit and in truth: for the Father seeketh such to worship him. God *is* a Spirit: and they that worship him must worship *him* in spirit and in truth."[217] Thus, a new covenant is required. A covenant that is not carnally based like that of the "Old Covenant," but one that is in "spirit and truth."

This is what John meant when he said that he "saw a new heaven and a new earth: for the first heaven and the first earth were passed away; and there was no more sea."[218] The "new earth" is a new set of God's people. They are His "Church,"

---

216 1 Cor. 6:19
217 Jhn. 4:23, 24
218 Rev. 21:1

they dwell in a "New Jerusalem," and they have a new name, "Christians."[219] The "new heaven" symbolizes a "New Covenant" that He makes with His new people. Thus, the Jews are replaced with "Christians," the Old Covenant is replaced with a "New Covenant," and the Old Jerusalem is replaced with a "New Jerusalem." In other words, the LORD "make all things new."[220]

While His people are in this "New Jerusalem," they are being trained to obey the laws and ordinances of this "New Covenant." This training consists of classwork based on the Bible and daily practice using biblical principles in their relationships with fellow Believers and non-Believers. This training is preparing them to dwell in Heaven, their future home.

The last state is becoming a spiritual being, with a glorified body,[221] and dwelling with God the Father, Jesus, and the Holy Ghost in Heaven. This final state happens after we have accepted Jesus as our LORD and savior, have been through the training program, and have passed through physical death.

---

219 Isa. 62:1–2, 65:15; Acts 11, 26; Rom. 9:26; 1 Pet. 2:9–10; Rev. 2:17, 3:12
220 Rev. 21:5
221 1 Cor. 15:35–58, Job 19:25–27

Chapter 12

Response to Promised Land Anxiety

In response to Abram's anxiety about the "Promised Land," the LORD cuts a "blood covenant" with him. No "blood covenant" is cut to address Abram's anxieties about the promises involving his "seed." These promises are based on the faith that Abram has in the LORD's Word and the faith that the LORD has in Abram's word. However, except for the cutting of a "blood covenant," the LORD follows a similar pattern: He confirms the promises, provides more details, and gives a vision of a future fulfillment.

Verse 9 reads, "And he said unto him, Take me an heifer of three years old, and a she goat of three years old, and a ram of three years old, and a turtledove, and a young pigeon. And he took unto him all these, and divided them in the midst, and laid each piece one against another: but the birds divided he not."[222]

The Animals

The animals named in verse 9 are also used for sacrificial offerings under the "Old Covenant." The LORD gives specific instructions for each type of offering: the burnt offerings,[223] the peace offerings,[224] the sin offering,[225] the guilt offerings,[226] etc. The LORD sometimes places blemish, age, and sex restrictions on these animals.[227] And, for some offerings, the LORD requires unbred animals. For these offerings, He directs the use of lambs,[228] kids,[229] and calves.[230] These terms refer to young, unbred sheep, goats, and cattle, respectively. Interestingly, the only restriction not placed on these animals is the blemish restriction.

---

222 Gen. 15:9–10
223 Lev. 1
224 Lev. 3
225 Lev. 4
226 Lev. 5:14–6:7
227 Lev. 1:3, 10; Exo. 12:5
228 Exo. 12:3–5; Lev. 5:1–6
229 Lev. 4:22–23, 5:1–6
230 Lev. 9:2;

The most notable requirement in Genesis 15:9 is the one requiring a three-year-old heifer. Heifers are normally young, female, unbred calves, not three-year-old-unbred, adult females.[231] Hence, the LORD requiring an adult female that is past her prime-breeding age is key to interpreting the symbolism in this verse. Moreover, the biblical symbolism of heifers and cows is broader than what we see in Genesis 15:9. (see Appendix III.)

The LORD requires two female animals: one barren (the heifer), the other not barren (the she-goat). Both females are three-year-old adults. He also requires a male animal (the ram). The ram is a three-year-old-adult male that has fathered an offspring. Besides the animals from the herd and the flock, the LORD requires two fowls: a turtledove and a young pigeon. The turtledove and pigeon are used under the "Old Covenant" as sacrificial offerings by the poor and for the purification of women after childbirth. Their use after childbirth prompts the conclusion that the fowls in this set of Scripture symbolize two birth events.

---

231 "Cattle Terminology: Bulls, Springers, Freemartins." Beef2Live. Accessed April 24, 2022. https://beef2live.com/story-cattle-terminology-bulls-springers-freemartins-85-103895.

The Dividing of the Animals

The heifer, the ram, and the she-goat are divided (cut into halves), but the fowls are not divided. The fowls are lain, intact, across from each other.[232] By dividing the heifer, the she-goat, and the ram, and then laying the intact fowls across from each other, the LORD forms two columns with a gap large enough for the "covenanters to pass between the parts."[233]

In this chapter, the dividing of the heifer, she-goat, and ram, and then laying the intact fowls across from each other are more than just protocol for cutting a "blood covenant." The arrangement, the animals, and the fowls depict two future prophetic events and the associated cast of characters. The two columns and fowls represent two future-prophetic birth events.

---

232 Gen. 15:10
233 John Gill's Commentary on Genesis 15:10

CHAPTER 13

The First Birth Event

The first birth event, depicted by the fowl and the first halves of the animals in the first column, occurs in Genesis chapter 16. In this chapter, we find Sarai, who is 76 years old, showing concern about her ability to bear a child. Because of her concern, she gives Hagar, her Egyptian handmaid,[234] to Abram so that she "may obtain children by her."[235] This results in Abram fathering a son and Hagar giving birth to that son, Ishmael. Sarai, however, remains barren.

By comparing the key relevant characteristics of the three-year-old she-goat with an offspring, the barren three-year-old heifer that is passed

---

234 Gen. 16:1
235 Gen. 16:2

prime-childbearing age, the ram with an offspring, with the key cast of characters in Genesis chapter 16: Hagar, Sarai, Abram, and Ishmael, we conclude that the first half of the three-year-old barren heifer is a metaphor for Sarai, the first half of the three-year-old she-goat is a metaphor for Hagar, and the first half of the three-year-old ram is a metaphor for Abram. Which fowl represents the birth of Ishmael and which represents a future second birth event is neither concluded nor proposed in this book. However, the fulfillment of the first prophetic event, the first half of the animals, is the birth of Ishmael in Genesis chapter 16.

CHAPTER 14

The Abram-Abraham Allegory

The identification of the symbolism of the animals is noteworthy. However, in Galatians chapter 4, Paul writes that the Abram-Abraham story is an allegory with a significant prophetic meaning. Thus, the animals are metaphors for characters that are also metaphors for a larger prophecy.

Paul writes, "For it is written, that Abraham had two sons, the one by a bondmaid, the other by a freewoman. But he who was of the bondwoman was born after the flesh; but he of the freewoman was by promise. Which things are an allegory: for these are the two covenants; the one from the mount Sinai, which gendereth to bondage, which is [Hagar]. For this [Hagar] is mount Sinai in Arabia, and answereth to Jerusalem which now is, and is in bondage with her children. But Jerusalem which is above is free, which is the mother of us all."[236]

Thus, Paul says that the Abram-Abraham story is a prophecy pointing to the establishment of the "Old" and "New Covenants," their corresponding "Holy Cities": Jerusalem and "New Jerusalem," and their citizenry symbolized by Ishmael and Isaac. Moreover, it points to the citizens of Jerusalem, the "Old Covenant" Jews that are "after the flesh," and to the citizens of the "New Jerusalem," the Christians that are spiritual and "by promise."

Therefore, the three-year-old barren heifer is a metaphor for Sarai, and Sarai is a metaphor for the barren "New Jerusalem" that is under the "New Covenant." The three-year-old she-goat is a metaphor for Hagar, and Hagar is a metaphor for the Jerusalem in Paul's day that is under the "Old Covenant" and is in bondage to the flesh. Ishmael is a metaphor for the citizens of the Jerusalem in Paul's day that are "after the flesh"; these are the "Old Covenant" Jews. Isaac is a metaphor for the citizens of the "New Jerusalem," that are "by promise"; these are the Christians.

---

236 Gal. 4:22–26

CHAPTER 15

The Second Birth Event

The Roles of the Cast of Characters

To utilize the metaphors in Genesis chapter 15 to identify the second event in the prophecy, we must identify what they symbolize and the characteristics of what they represent. First, the three-year-old ram is a metaphor for Abram, and Abram has a covenant relationship with Sarai. In Genesis chapter 16, however, Abram enters into a covenant relationship with Hagar. Thus, in Genesis chapter 16, Abram becomes the husband to both Sarai and Hagar. Moreover, Abram is a forerunner to Abraham, he is the father of Ishmael, and he is the LORD's representative on earth. Therefore, Abram's roles are that of a husband, a father, a forerunner, and the LORD's representative on earth.

Second, we have the three-year-old she-goat. It is a metaphor for Hagar, and Hagar is a metaphor for the Jerusalem of Paul's day that is under the "Old Covenant" and is in bondage to the flesh. Hagar is Sarai's maidservant, she is an Egyptian, and she enters into a covenant relationship (a marriage type relationship) with Abram. This marriage type relationship results in a son named Ishmael, and Ishmael is a metaphor for the citizens of the Jerusalem of Paul's day that are in bondage to the flesh. Therefore, Hagar's role is that of a carnal "Holy City" of the LORD, Jerusalem, that is in bondage to the flesh, and Ishmael's role is that of citizens of a "Holy City" that will fall in bondage to the flesh.

By using Paul's allegorical interpretation of the Abram-Abraham story, by looking at the characteristics of Abram and Hagar, by noting that the fowls mark birth events, and by noting how the LORD defines "Holy Cities" as anywhere He places His Temple and "cause his name to dwell,"[237] I concluded that the second event, depicted by a fowl and the second halves of the animals that are in the second column, is the establishment of the "Old Covenant" at Mount Sinai and the birth of the Children of Israel under the "Old Covenant." The second event occurs in Exodus chapter 24

---

237 Deu. 12:11

when the "Old Covenant" terms are read, and the Children of Israel agree to them.[238]

To advance our understanding of the symbolism, we must explore what else happens when the Children of Israel are born under the "Old Covenant." For instance, they are given judges to administer the laws.[239] They are given a mobile "Tabernacle in the Wilderness"[240] to represent the LORD's presence with them, to serve as a Temple for performing sacrifices, and to be the place where the LORD chooses "to cause his name to dwell."[241] They are dwelling together exclusively with the LORD. Moreover, they are given Priests for the duties of the "Tabernacle in the Wilderness."[242]

Thus, when the Children of Israel are born under the "Old Covenant" at Mount Sinai, the LORD gives them the infrastructure for the establishment of a city.[243] And not just any city, the LORD provides them the infrastructure that gives birth

---

238 Exo. 24:7
239 Exo. 18
240 Exo. 25–27
241 Deu. 12:10–14
242 Exo. 28–29
243 Drane, John. "City - Definition, Meaning & Synonyms." Vocabulary.com. Accessed April 24, 2022. https://www.vocabulary.com/dictionary/city.

to a "Holy City."[244] Consequently, the Children of Israel born under the "Old Covenant" are citizens of this "Holy City." Their birth is symbolized by either the pigeon or the turtledove. However, just as Ishmael symbolizes the citizens of Jerusalem in Paul's day, Ishmael also symbolizes the Children of Israel born under the "Old Covenant" at Mount Sinai.

This "Holy City" and the Children of Israel born under the "Old Covenant" at Mount Sinai are in bondage "after the flesh," and they will ultimately become the Jerusalem and the "Old Covenant" Jews that are prophesied through Hagar and Ishmael. Therefore, the second half of the three-year-old she-goat is a metaphor for this carnal "Holy City."

Though this "Holy City" will become the Jerusalem referred to by Paul, it is not yet located in Jerusalem, which is a single geographic location on the earth. The "Holy City" born at Mount Sinai is mobile and physically moves with the Children of Israel as they wander in the wilderness for forty years. This is because the "Tabernacle in the Wilderness," the Temple, moves with them. However, after they enter the "Promised Land," the LORD declares that His "Holy City" will be at

---

244 Deu. 12:10–14

a single geographic location within the territory of Benjamin,[245] and it will be in the physical city of Jerusalem.

Moreover, when this carnal "Holy City" is established at Mount Sinai, the barren spiritual "Holy City" is also present. This is because the barren spiritual "Holy City" is symbolized by Sarai, and Sarai is present when Hagar gives birth to Ishmael. Sarah, who follows Sarai, will not give birth to Isaac until later, and his birth is not included in the Genesis chapter 15 prophecy. However, Isaac's birth is not only a metaphor for the birth of the Christians in the NT, it is also a metaphor for the new Children of Israel born in the wilderness. And for a time period, the new Children of Israel born in the wilderness and the Children of Israel that came out of Egypt are coexisting in the wilderness. This is as Ishmael and Isaac did and as the "Old Covenant" Jews and the Christians did. Nevertheless, after forty years of wandering in the wilderness, the new Children of Israel enter the "Promised Land," and the Children of Israel that came out of Egypt die in the wilderness.

Consequently, Sarai, who is barren when Hagar gives birth to Ishmael, will, through Sarah, have more children than Hagar. In other words, "New

---

245 Jos. 18:28

Jerusalem" will have more citizens than Jerusalem. Paul writes, "Rejoice, thou barren that bearest not; break forth and cry, thou that travailest not: for the desolate hath many more children than she which hath an husband."[246] The second half of the three-year-old barren heifer is a metaphor for the barren spiritual "Holy City" present at Mount Sinai. And based on Exodus chapters 19-24, Acts chapter 2, and Jasher 82:6, both the carnal and spiritual "Holy Cities" give birth to their firstborn on the same "Appointed Day," the "Feast of Weeks." This "Appointed Day" is called the "Day of Pentecost" in the Book of Acts.

Mount Sinai is a Type of Wedding Ceremony

The Characters and the Process
The establishment of the "Old Covenant" at Mount Sinai is a type of wedding ceremony. In this wedding ceremony, Jesus is the Groom, and Moses is His earthly representative. The "Bride" is the "Holy City." Jesus is charged by "God the Father" with obeying and training up his "Bride" and His children in the laws and ordinances of the marriage covenant. The children are the citizens of the "Holy City," and the marriage covenant is the "Old Covenant."

---

246 Gal. 4:27

The Bible describes this wedding ceremony in Exodus chapters 19–24. We observe the reading of the wedding vows and their acceptance in Exodus 24:7, "And he took the book of the covenant, and read in the audience of the people: and they said, All that the LORD hath said will we do, and be obedient."[247]

And, just as in most weddings, the Groom is present; Jesus is also present at Mount Sinai. "Then went up Moses, and Aaron, Nadab, and Abihu, and seventy of the elders of Israel: And they saw the God of Israel: and there was under his feet as it were a paved work of a sapphire stone, and as it were the body of heaven in his clearness."[248] Jesus is the "God of Israel" they saw, and He is the true Husband in Heaven and in earth. This was established in the Garden of Eden. Moses only serves as Jesus' earthly representative.

The New Testament Meaning

This earthly type marriage of Moses to the "Holy City" parallels the marriage of Abram to Hagar, and it points to the marriage of John the Baptist to the "Old Covenant" Jews in Jerusalem. In each case, we have a man taking a wife that is not of his kindred, not of his nature, and they do not share

---

247 Exo. 24:7
248 Exo. 24:9–10

the same father. This situation also applies to the marriage of Jesus and the "Holy City" at Mount Sinai.

To elaborate, Jesus is a spiritual being, but His marriage at Mount Sinai is to a carnal city and a carnal people. They are "unequally yoked together,"[249] and the marriage does not last. The "Holy City" and the "Children of Israel" will break the covenant of marriage, the "Old Covenant," and crucify their Godly Husband, Jesus, on the cross. Thereby, as Paul writes in Romans 7: 1–4, Jesus, in the spirit, is free to take another wife; the Children of Israel that accepts Jesus are also free to take another husband; and this is what Jesus and the Believing "Old Covenant" Jews do in the NT.

In the NT, Jesus takes a new "Bride," the "New Jerusalem," and they marry under a "New Covenant" and have a new set of Children called "Christians." These first Christians are Believing "Old Covenant" Jews. And according to Acts 11:26, they "were called Christians first in Antioch." This marriage in the NT is outside the scope of this chapter because it is symbolized by the marriage of Abraham and Sarah. However, a noteworthy point that should be made is that Abraham

---

249 2 Cor. 6:14

and Sarah are of the same kindred, nature, and they share the same father, Terah.[250] Abraham makes this point when he tells Abimelech in Genesis chapter 20 that Sarah "*is* my sister; she *is* the daughter of my father, but not the daughter of my mother; and she became my wife."[251] Thus, Sarah was Abraham's sister and spouse.

The marriages between Abram and Hagar, Moses and the carnal "Holy City" at Mount Sinai, and John the Baptist and Jerusalem are between husbands and wives that do not share the same kindred, nature, and father. However, the marriages between Abraham and Sarah, Joshua and the Israelites that enter the "Promised Land," and Jesus and "New Jerusalem" are between husbands and wives that share the same kindred, nature, and father. Paul and Jesus stress the meaning behind this difference.

For some, the difference between having Abram as your father and having Abraham as your father is "a distinction without a difference." However, in the Book of John, chapter 8, Jesus makes a distinction. In John chapter 8, the Pharisees tell Jesus that "We be Abraham's seed."[252] Jesus responds

---

250 Gen. 11:27
251 Gen. 20:12
252 Jhn. 8:33

to them by referencing the story of Ishmael and Isaac. He says that "the servant abideth not in the house for ever: *but* the Son abideth ever."[253] This is a reference to Ishmael and Isaac, who both, for a period of time, "abideth" in the house with Abraham. However, Ishmael is cast out when he is approximately 19 years old.[254] Isaac, however, "abideth ever."

Later in verse 39, the Pharisees reiterate that their father is Abraham. This time Jesus states that "If ye were Abraham's children, ye would do the works of Abraham. But now ye seek to kill me, a man that hath told you the truth, which I have heard of God: this did not Abraham. Ye do the deeds of your father."[255]

The Pharisees, wanting to continue this discourse, then declare that they "be not born of fornication; we have one Father, even God. Jesus said unto them, If God were your Father, ye would love me: for I proceeded forth and came from God; neither came I of myself, but he sent me. Why do ye not understand my speech? even because ye cannot hear my word. Ye are of your father the devil, and the lusts of your father ye will do. He was a

---

253 Jhn. 8:35
254 Gen. 21:9–15; Jasher 21:11–16
255 Jhn. 8:39–41

murderer from the beginning, and abode not in the truth, because there is no truth in him. When he speaketh a lie, he speaketh of his own: for he is a liar, and the father of it.[256] Thus, Jesus is making clear that He and the Pharisees do not share the same Father, and their father is not Abraham.

However, at the tomb, Jesus makes clear that He and His "Bride" under the "New Covenant" share the same Father and the same God. At the tomb, Jesus tells Mary, who is a future citizen of the "New Jerusalem," to "go to my brethren, and say unto them, I ascend unto my Father, and your Father; and to my God, and your God."[257] Thus, He shares the same Father and God as the citizens of the "New Jerusalem." This is prophesied in the marriage of Abraham and Sarah. Jesus marries His half-sister, "New Jerusalem," and Jesus is our Elder Brother.

This marriage of Jesus to the "New Jerusalem" is depicted in the Book of Revelation when John says that he "saw the holy city, new Jerusalem, coming down from God out of heaven, prepared as a bride adorned for her husband."[258] It is also depicted in the Book of the Song of Solomon. The

---

256 Jhn. 8:41–44
257 Jhn. 20:17
258 Rev. 21:2

Song of Solomon, which is a metaphor for Jesus' love for His "Bride," foretells Jesus calling His "Bride" "my sister, my spouse."[259] As Christians, this is why we refer to each other as brothers and sisters—we share the same Heavenly Father, and Jesus is our Elder Brother.

The idea that Jesus is our Elder Brother may also explain our observation in Genesis chapters 1-3. We noted that Abraham, Isaac, and Jacob only knew the God in Genesis Chapter 1 by His title, and we learn in Exodus 6:3 that this was intentional. However, Abraham, Isaac, and Jacob knew the name of their Elder Brother Jesus, which is JEHOVAH. This is very similar to how we operate today in our culture.

We know the names of our siblings, and we casually and frequently call our siblings by their names. However, we do not call our father by his name. Moreover, there may be years before we even know our father's name. We simply call our father by his titles: father, daddy, dad, etc. This behavior, or cultural norm, is also noted in Jesus. Jesus, while walking on earth, never refers to His Father by His name. He only refers to His Father by His title, Father.

---

[259] Son. 4:9–12; Son. 5:1

CHAPTER 16

The Name Change

Though some may see the name change in Genesis chapter 17 as merely the LORD confirming to Abram that He will make him "a father of many nations."[260] Similarly, they believe that the name change is to confirm to Sarai that she will "be a mother of nations; kings of people shall be of her."[261] This name change, however, has a prophetic meaning too. The LORD also uses this name change to prophesy a future change in the role, the person, or the people. This will now be explained.

According to Paul, Abram's descendants that come out of physical bondage in Egypt and are brought under the "Old Covenant" at Mount Sinai will

---

260 Gen. 17:5
261 Gen. 17:16

symbolically have the bondage nature of Ishmael, Abram's son by Hagar, the Egyptian woman.[262] The LORD sends Moses, in a "Forerunner" role, to lead these descendants of Abram out of bondage in Egypt and into the wilderness. However, neither they nor Moses is allowed to go into the "Promised Land." Thus, we have a "forerunner": Moses, leading one set of Abram's descendants out of Egypt; bringing them under the "Old Covenant"; and, then, due to their disobedience, not being allowed to enter the "Promised Land."

The LORD makes clear that the descendants of Abram that come out of Egypt under Moses die in the Wilderness and do not enter the "Promised Land."[263] The descendants that enter the "Promised Land" are born in the Wilderness and are circumcised after entering the "Promised Land."[264] And, though this was not the establishment of the "New Covenant," the circumcision after entering the "Promised Land" points to the "New Covenant" being established with a new people. These descendants are symbolized by Isaac, who is born of Abraham and Sarah, not Abram and Sarai. The LORD sends a second

---

262 Gal. 4:21–26
263 Num. 32:11–12, Jos. 5:6
264 Num. 32:11–12, Jos. 5:7

leader, Joshua, in a "Fulfiller" role, to lead this second set of people into the "Promised Land."

Therefore, in the allegorized stories of Abram-Abraham and Moses-Joshua, there are corresponding roles. Abram and Moses have corresponding roles. Hagar and the carnal "Holy City" established at Mount Sinai under the "Old Covenant" have corresponding roles.[265] Ishmael and the Children of Israel born under the "Old Covenant" at Mount Sinai have corresponding roles.[266] Sarai and the barren spiritual "Holy City" at Mount Sinai have corresponding roles.[267] Abraham and Joshua have corresponding roles. Sarah and the metaphorical spiritual "Holy City" born in the Wilderness have corresponding roles.[268] And, finally, Isaac and the Children of Israel that are born in the Wilderness and enter the "Promised Land" have corresponding roles.[269] Thus, the second half of the three-year-old ram is a metaphor for Moses.

Therefore, God uses the name change to foretell that He will send two sets of leaders, and He will have two sets of people. The first leader, a "Forerunner," will lead the first set of God's

---

265 Gal. 4:21–25
266 Gal. 4:21–25
267 Gal. 4:21–31
268 Gal. 4:21–31
269 Gal. 4:21–31

people out of bondage and into the Wilderness. However, the "Forerunner" will not lead this first set of people into the "Promised Land." A second leader, a "Fulfiller," will come. He will lead a second set of people, plus a remnant of the first set, into the "Promised Land." In the story of Moses-Joshua, the remnant that exits Egypt and enters the "Promised Land" is Joshua and Caleb.[270]

The LORD limits the symbolism of the "blood covenant" cut in Genesis chapter 15 to the birth of Ishmael and the cutting of the "Old Covenant" at Mount Sinai. The symbolism does not apply to events after the name change of Abram and Sarai. In other words, Abraham, Sarah, and Isaac are not included.

Repeating and Expanding (Telescoping)

The birth of the Israelites under the "Old Covenant" occurs 422 years after the cutting of the covenant in Genesis chapter 15 and 400 years after the birth of Isaac.[271] The establishment of the "Old Covenant" is part of a story that starts with the exodus from Egypt and ends with the entry into the "Promised Land." This story follows a biblical pattern of repeating and expanding.

---

270 Num. 32:11–12
271 A detailed discussion is in chapter 20

For example, the allegorized story of Abram-Abraham has prophetic meaning for key people and events in the NT. Similarly, the allegorized story of Moses-Joshua has prophetic meaning for the same key people and events in the NT. These key people and events are Jesus, John the Baptist, and the events involving their stories.

And, since the Abram-Abraham and Moses-Joshua allegories point to the same events and people in the NT, both allegories should have similarities in their cast of characters and events—and they do. There are, however, differences. The Moses-Joshua allegory provides more details than the Abram-Abraham allegory. This is the case, in general, for OT allegories. Each succeeding OT allegory will provide more details than the preceding OT allegory.

For example, in the Abram-Abraham allegory, the change from Abram to Abraham and Sarai to Sarah identifies a change, but the prophetic meaning for the change is not revealed. The prophetic meaning of the name change is not revealed until the Moses-Joshua story. In the Moses-Joshua story, we learn that there will be two leaders, a "Forerunner" and a "Fulfiller," and they will not share the same body. Moreover, the Abram-Abraham allegory provides no indication that any remnant of Ishmael will join Isaac in receiving the promises that the LORD made to Abraham. However, in the Moses-Joshua allegory, we read that a small remnant that exits Egypt, Caleb and Joshua, will also enter the "Promised Land."

Like the Abram-Abraham allegory, the Moses-Joshua allegory foretells that God will send a "Forerunner" to lead one set of people out of a spiritual Egypt and into a spiritual wilderness. God will then send a "Fulfiller" to lead a second set of God's people, plus a remnant of the first set, out of the spiritual wilderness and into a spiritual "Promised Land." We would not have discovered this prophecy without the added details of the second allegory.

The two leaders in the NT corresponds to John the Baptist, the "Forerunner," and Jesus, the "Fulfiller." The spiritual Egypt is Jerusalem.[272] The covenant cut is the "Covenant of Water Baptism." The wilderness is the wilderness used by John the Baptist to train and baptize his set of people. The spiritual "Promised Land" is "New Jerusalem," and Jesus leads His set of people to "New Jerusalem." There is, however, a remnant of "Old Covenant" Jews and followers of John the Baptist that will enter "New Jerusalem." Jesus uses these "Old Covenant"

---

272 Rev. 11:8

Jews and the followers of John the Baptist to build His "Church." In fact, the twelve Apostles chosen by Jesus are Believing "Old Covenant" Jews.

The Overall Symbolism

The turtledove and pigeon symbolize the births of Ishmael and the Children of Israel born under the "Old Covenant" at Mount Sinai. They are also citizens of the carnal "Holy City" established at Mount Sinai. Half of the she-goat symbolizes Hagar; the other half symbolizes the carnal "Holy City" under the "Old Covenant" and was established at Mount Sinai. Half of the heifer symbolizes Sarai; the other half symbolizes the barren spiritual "Holy City" that is present at the establishment of the "Old Covenant." Half of the ram symbolizes Abram; the other half symbolizes Moses.

CHAPTER 17

Forerunner Similarities

The similarities in the roles that Abram and Moses play in their respective stories are repeated in the Bible. This role is that of a forerunner. Abram is a forerunner to Abraham, just as Moses is a forerunner to Joshua. Jacob is a forerunner to Israel, just as Elijah is a forerunner to Elisha. And, in the NT, John the Baptist is the ultimate forerunner to Jesus.

A phenomenon of OT forerunners is that their human remains are not accessible after they complete their missions. For example, Abram stops existing after becoming Abraham. Jacob stops existing after becoming Israel. "Moses the servant of the LORD died there in the land of Moab, according to the word of the LORD. And he buried him in a valley in the land of Moab, over against

Bethpeor: but no man knoweth of his sepulchre unto this day."[273]

Elijah, a forerunner to Elisha, "went up by a whirlwind into heaven. And Elisha saw it, and he cried, My father, my father, the chariot of Israel, and the horsemen thereof. And he saw him no more: and he took hold of his own clothes, and rent them in two pieces."[274] Similarly in the NT, John the Baptist's "disciples came, and took up the body, and buried it."[275] However, the location of his grave is uncertain.

A second similarity of forerunners is that they do not carnally experience the fulfillment of the promises. They "died in faith, not having received the promises, but having seen them afar off, and were persuaded of them, and embraced them, and confessed that they were strangers and pilgrims on the earth."[276] In the case of Abram, he did not experience the birth of the "Son of Promise," Isaac. Abraham and Sarah experienced the birth of the "Son of Promise." This is because Abram and Sarai cease to exist when Abraham and Sarah came into existence in Genesis

---

273 Deu. 34:5–6
274 2 Kin. 2:11–12
275 Matt. 14:12
276 Heb. 11:13

chapter 17, and Isaac is born in Genesis chapter 21. However, Jesus says that "Abraham rejoiced to see my day: and he saw it, and was glad."[277] When and how Jesus shows Abram-Abraham His day is not explicitly stated in the written Scriptures. Nevertheless, we know that Abram-Abraham sees Jesus' day because Jesus said that he did.

The seeing of Jesus' day begs the question: Did Abram-Abraham believe that if "God the Father" would one day raise His only begotten Son up from the dead, will He also raise up his own only son,[278] Isaac, from the dead too? The Book of Hebrews addresses this question this way, "By faith Abraham, when he was tried, offered up Isaac: and he that had received the promises offered up his only begotten son, Of whom it was said, That in Isaac shall thy seed be called: Accounting that God was able to raise him up, even from the dead; from whence also he received him in a figure."[279]

With Moses, he prays that the LORD will allow him to go over into the "Promised Land." He prays, "Let me go over, and see the good land that is beyond Jordan, that goodly mountain, and

---

277 Jhn. 8:56
278 Gen. 22:2
279 Heb. 11:17–19

Lebanon."[280] But Moses states that "the LORD was wroth with me for your sakes, and would not hear me: and the LORD said unto me, Let it suffice thee; speak no more unto me of this matter. Get thee up into the top of Pisgah, and lift up thine eyes westward, and northward, and southward, and eastward, and behold it with thine eyes: for thou shalt not go over this Jordan. But charge Joshua, and encourage him, and strengthen him: for he shall go over before this people, and he shall cause them to inherit the land which thou shalt see."[281]

Jacob, like Abram and Moses, is not given possession of the "Promised Land." The LORD only allows Jacob to see the land. Moreover, the LORD gives Jacob a vision of Jesus' day. We read in Genesis chapter 28 that Jacob "dreamed, and behold a ladder set up on the earth, and the top of it reached to heaven: and behold the angels of God ascending and descending on it. And, behold, the LORD stood above it, and said, I am the LORD God of Abraham thy father, and the God of Isaac: the land whereon thou liest, to thee will I give it, and to thy seed; And thy seed shall be as the dust of the earth, and thou shalt spread abroad to the west, and to the east, and to the north, and to the south: and in thee and in thy seed shall all the

---

280 Deu. 3:25
281 Deu. 3:26–28

families of the earth be blessed. And, behold, I am with thee, and will keep thee in all places whither thou goest, and will bring thee again into this land; for I will not leave thee, until I have done that which I have spoken to thee of."[282]

Jesus references this dream by Jacob in the NT when He says, "Verily, verily, I say unto you, Hereafter ye shall see heaven open, and the angels of God ascending and descending upon the Son of man."[283] Jacob's dream came before the LORD changes his name to Israel. The dream occurs in Genesis chapter 28, and the LORD changes Jacob's name to Israel in Genesis chapter 32.

They Were Pursued and Persecuted

There are two key subplots in the story of Moses-Joshua that do not have parallels in the story of Abram-Abraham. These two subplots add information. The first involves the Pharaoh and "six hundred chosen chariots, and all the chariots of Egypt, and captains over every one of them"[284] pursuing the Children of Israel after they leave Egypt. However, while pursuing them, "the LORD overthrew the Egyptians in the midst of the sea.

---

282 Gen. 28:12–15
283 Jhn. 1:51
284 Exo. 14:7

And the waters returned, and covered the chariots, and the horsemen, and all the host of Pharaoh that came into the sea after them; there remained not so much as one of them."[285]

The second subplot involves the group of people that came out of Egypt with Moses, but they carry the spiritual bondage of Egypt with them. This is the group of people who said to Moses when they saw Egyptians pursuing them that "because there were no graves in Egypt, hast thou taken us away to die in the wilderness? wherefore hast thou dealt thus with us, to carry us forth out of Egypt? Is not this the word that we did tell thee in Egypt, saying, Let us alone, that we may serve the Egyptians? For it had been better for us to serve the Egyptians, than that we should die in the wilderness."[286]

This is the same group of people that "saw that Moses delayed to come down out of the mount, the people gathered themselves together unto Aaron, and said unto him, Up, make us gods, which shall go before us; for as for this Moses, the man that brought us up out of the land of Egypt, we wot not what is become of him."[287] Moses physically led

---

285 Exo. 14: 27, 28
286 Exo. 14:11–12
287 Exo. 32:1

this group of people out of Egypt, but he was not able to spiritually lead the Egypt out of this group of people.

The identified two subplots are allegorical prophecies that are realized in the NT in the story of John the Baptist. The Pharaoh and the Egyptians seek to destroy Moses and the Children of Israel. And they would have, if the LORD had not intervened. Similarly, King Herod and the Jewish leadership in Jerusalem seek to destroy and persecute John the Baptist and his followers. And like the Children of Israel, John the Baptist and his followers are in bondage to King Herod and the Jewish leadership until they leave Jerusalem and dwell in the wilderness.

Like the Pharaoh and the Egyptians, the Jewish leaders pursue John the Baptist and his followers into the wilderness to harass and to challenge him.[288] King Herod eventually beheads John the Baptist,[289] and many of John the Baptist's followers shift to following Jesus. However, the persecution significantly increases. The Jewish leadership uses the Romans to crucify Jesus, they stone Stephen to death, and their persecution drives the Christians out of Jerusalem. The LORD,

---

288 Matt. 3:7
289 Matt. 14:1-12

however, will later send the Roman army to destroy Jerusalem in AD 70.[290]

Many Are Called, But Few Are Chosen

Concerning the second point, there are some that came out of Jerusalem with John the Baptist carrying the spiritual bondage of an apostatized form of Judaism. These people are among all the others that are led into the wilderness by John the Baptist to be prepared for entry into the spiritual "Promised Land." John the Baptist teaches them about the Kingdom of God and heaven, and he baptizes them "with water unto repentance."[291]

However, these people have a form of Christianity. Some have the name "Christian" but are attempting to align the teaching of the "New Covenant" to fit their apostatized form of Judaism. Moreover, they lack the baptism of the Holy Spirit and fire. For example, one of the most challenging issues is the requirement for circumcision. Jesus addresses their behavior when he says, "No man putteth a piece of new cloth unto an old garment, for that which is put in to fill it up taketh from

---

290 Schäfer, Peter (2003). The History of the Jews in the Greco-Roman World: The Jews of Palestine from Alexander the Great to the Arab. Conquest Routledge. pp. 129–130. ISBN 9781134403172.

291 Matt. 3:11

the garment, and the rent is made worse. Neither do men put new wine into old bottles: else the bottles break, and the wine runneth out, and the bottles perish: but they put new wine into new bottles, and both are preserved."[292] The LORD uses Paul to address a great deal of this apostasy in his day. However, there are still people from the carnal "seed" of Abram and Hagar practicing an apostatized form of the "New Covenant" and Christianity still among us today.

Jesus also refers to this carnal "seed" of Abram and Hagar in "The Parable of the Wedding Feast."[293] Jesus said, "When the king came in to see the guests, he saw there a man which had not on a wedding garment: And he saith unto him, Friend, how camest thou in hither not having a wedding garment? And he was speechless. Then said the king to the servants, Bind him hand and foot, and take him away, and cast him into outer darkness; there shall be weeping and gnashing of teeth. For many are called, but few are chosen."[294]

Many are called out of the NT Jerusalem. Some of them, however, are clothed in their old ways and traditions. They want to bring these old ways and

---

292 Matt. 9:16–17
293 Matt. 22:1–14
294 Matt. 22:11–14

traditions with them into the new, but this is unacceptable. They only had the baptism of John the Baptist; they were not baptized "with the Holy Ghost, and with fire"[295] that John the Baptist said Jesus would do for them.

This is also illustrated in "The Parable of the Ten Virgins." In this parable, ten virgins, while waiting for their bridegroom to come, take their lamps to meet their bridegroom. "And five of them were wise, and five were foolish. They that were foolish took their lamps, and took no oil with them: But the wise took oil in their vessels with their lamps. While the bridegroom tarried, they all slumbered and slept. And at midnight there was a cry made, Behold, the bridegroom cometh; go ye out to meet him."[296]

"Then all those virgins arose, and trimmed their lamps. And the foolish said unto the wise, Give us of your oil; for our lamps are gone out. But the wise answered, saying, Not so; lest there be not enough for us and you: but go ye rather to them that sell, and buy for yourselves. And while they went to buy, the bridegroom came; and they that were ready went in with him to the marriage: and the door was shut. Afterward came also the other

---

295 Matt. 3:11
296 Matt. 25:2–6

virgins, saying, Lord, Lord, open to us. But he answered and said, Verily I say unto you, I know you not."[297]

In this parable, the "oil" represents the Holy Spirit. Thus, the five foolish virgins lack the Holy Spirit. Water Baptism is not enough; we will simply be a lamp without oil. We should also allow God to fill our bodies with the Holy Spirit by being baptized of the Holy Spirit and fire by Jesus. Moreover, we must allow the Holy Spirit to work within us and not just reside within us. We note that the five wise "virgins arose, and trimmed their lamps."[298]

Thus, the oil is not just residing in their lamps; the oil is burning in their lamps. The Holy Spirit should work within us to guide our decision making, our conversation, and our daily behavior. Paul said in the Book of Ephesians to "grieve not the holy Spirit of God, whereby ye are sealed unto the day of redemption."[299]

The LORD will choose the few that come in their new wedding garments and with their lamb filled with oil that is burning. These gave up their old ways and traditions, they received the Water

---

[297] Matt. 25:7–12
[298] Matt. 25:7
[299] Eph. 4:30

Baptism unto repentance from John the Baptist, and they accepted the new teachings, doctrines, and the baptism of the Holy Spirit from Jesus.

Hence, John the Baptist is not able to provide all that is needed to enter into the kingdom of Heaven. John the Baptist is able to baptize in the Jordan River, but he is not able to symbolically take them across the Jordan River. Someone greater than him has to come after him to provide what he cannot provide. This task would fall into the hands of Jesus, and John the Baptist understood this. John the Baptist said, "[Jesus] must increase, but I must decrease."[300]

Similarly, just as Moses is charged by the LORD to anoint Joshua to lead the Children of Israel into the "Promised Land," the LORD charges John the Baptist to anoint Jesus to lead the children of His Kingdom into His spiritual "Promised Land." We read in the Book of Numbers that, "the LORD said unto Moses, Take thee Joshua the son of Nun, a man in whom is the spirit, and lay thine hand upon him; And set him before Eleazar the priest, and before all the congregation; and give him a charge in their sight. And thou shalt put some of

---

[300] Jhn. 3:30

thine honour upon him, that all the congregation of the children of Israel may be obedient."[301]

In the case of John the Baptist, he is charged with baptizing Jesus. This was something that he felt unworthy to do. However, Jesus tells him, "Suffer it to be so now: for thus it becometh us to fulfil all righteousness. Then he suffered him."[302] In other words, Jesus is saying this is prophesied; just as Moses is charged by the LORD to anoint Joshua, and Elijah is charged by the LORD to anoint Elisha, you, John the Baptist, must anoint Me to fulfill this prophecy.

---

301 Num. 27:18–20
302 Matt. 3:15

Chapter 18

Numbering the Children of Israel

Numbered after the Exodus

In Genesis 15:5, the LORD tells Abram to "look now toward heaven, and tell the stars, if thou be able to number them: and he said unto him, So shall thy seed be."[303] Thus, He tells Abram that just as he is unable to number the stars, he will not be able to number his future "seed." This is referenced in the Book of Revelation, "I beheld, and, lo, a great multitude, which no man could number, of all nations, and kindreds, and people, and tongues, stood before the throne, and before the Lamb, clothed with white robes, and palms in their hands."[304]

---

303 Gen. 15:5
304 Rev. 7:9

The LORD begins numbering the people associated with Abram when he exits Egypt in Genesis chapter 12. There are four: Abram, Sarai, Lot, and Hagar. And, though the "seed" of Abram that come out of Egypt in the Book of Exodus are "as the stars of heaven for multitude,"[305] they are numbered. We read that "the children of Israel journeyed from Rameses to Succoth, about six hundred thousand on foot that were men, beside children."[306]

In the Book of Numbers, the LORD tells Moses to number all men "twenty years old and upward, all that are able to go forth to war in Israel."[307] In doing this, the LORD makes known that the Israelites that came out of Egypt and went under the "Old Covenant" are not the ultimate fulfillment of the promise that He made to Abram. These Israelites pointed to the Children of Israel that will be of the physical "seed" of Abram, but not of the spiritual "seed" of Abraham. However, from this physical "seed" would come a very small number that will be born again in the spirit of Abraham and Sarah, and they will produce a spiritual "seed" that "no man could number."[308]

---

305 Deu. 1:10
306 Exo. 12:37
307 Num. 1:3
308 Rev. 7:9

The "Numbered" Produced the Innumerable

Of all the Children of Israel that came out of Egypt with Moses and were born into the "Old Covenant," only Caleb and Joshua will be born again in the spirit of Abraham and Sarah, will survive the forty years in the wilderness, and will dwell in the "Promised Land." The LORD declares this after the evil report from the men that Moses sent to "spy out the land of Canaan"[309] causes murmuring among the Children of Israel "against Moses and against Aaron."[310]

"Moses sent [twelve men] to search the land, who returned, and made all the congregation to murmur against him, by bringing up a slander upon the land, Even those men that did bring up the evil report upon the land, died by the plague before the LORD. But Joshua the son of Nun, and Caleb the son of Jephunneh, which were of the men that went to search the land, lived still."[311] The LORD declares, "surely none of the men that came up out of Egypt, from twenty years old and upward, shall see the land which I sware unto Abraham, unto Isaac, and unto Jacob; because they have not wholly followed me: Save Caleb the son of

---

309 Num. 13:17
310 Num. 14:2
311 Num. 14:36–38

Jephunneh the Kenezzite, and Joshua the son of Nun: for they have wholly followed the LORD."[312]

But as for those under the age of twenty, the LORD allows them to enter the "Promised Land." The LORD states that "your little ones, which ye said should be a prey, and your children, which in that day had no knowledge between good and evil, they shall go in thither, and unto them will I give it, and they shall possess it."[313] Thus, the LORD treats them in a similar manner as He treated Adam and Eve—innocent and not knowing the difference between good and evil.

Caleb and Joshua, who are over twenty years of age, enter the "Promised Land" because they believe and are born again in the spirit of Abraham and Sarah. They symbolize the "Old Covenant" dead saints that are referenced in Ezekiel chapter 37, Matthew chapter 27, Hosea chapter 6, 1 Corinthians chapter 15, and in Revelation chapters 7 and 14. These dead saints are the 144,000 in Revelation 7:1–8. They are the "firstfruits" in Revelation 14:4. They are the ones prophesied in Hosea chapter 6 to be revived two days after Jesus' death on the cross and be raised up three

---

312 Num. 32:11–12
313 Deu. 1:39

days later with and after Jesus.[314] In addition, Paul said in 1 Corinthians chapter 15 that Jesus is "the firstfruits of them that slept."[315] We note that Paul did not say of them that sleep; he said "of them that slept," past tense. Thus, the dead saints were no longer sleeping. They are raised from the grave with him on the "Feast of Firstfruit."

This small-numbered group from "the whole house of Israel"[316] is the "Old Covenant" saints that died before Jesus' death and resurrection. And, after their resurrection, they "went into the holy city, and [they] appeared unto many."[317] Afterward, these once dead saints ascend in the cloud with Jesus.[318] We read in Ephesians chapter 4 that "when [Jesus] ascended up on high, he led captivity captive, and gave gifts unto men."[319] These captives that He led up with Him are the dead saints that were held captive by the grave.

Numbered Producing Innumerable Repeated

The pattern of the LORD using a very small-numbered group to produce an innumerable group is

---

314 Hos. 6:2
315 1 Cor. 15:20
316 Eze. 37:11
317 Matt. 27:53
318 Acts 1:9
319 Eph. 4:8

repeated many times in the Bible. For example, in 1 Peter we read that "once the longsuffering of God waited in the days of Noah, while the ark was a preparing, wherein few, that is, eight souls were saved by water."[320] The LORD used these eight souls to repopulate the earth and to build to Himself a nation that "no man could number."

Moreover, the LORD reveals to Nebuchadnezzar in a dream the four future Gentile nations that will rule over the Children of Israel. Nebuchadnezzar "sawest that the stone was cut out of the mountain without hands, and that it brake in pieces the iron, the brass, the clay, the silver, and the gold."[321] Nebuchadnezzar sees this "stone that smote the image [become] a great mountain, and filled the whole earth."[322] This stone symbolizes how "the God of heaven [would] set up a kingdom, which shall never be destroyed: and the kingdom shall not be left to other people, but it shall break in pieces and consume all these kingdoms, and it shall stand for ever."[323]

This stone points to the 120 souls that are in the upper room on the "Day of Pentecost,"[324] and

---

320 1 Pet. 3:20
321 Dan. 2:45
322 Dan. 2:35
323 Dan. 2:44
324 Acts 1:12–15

the mountain that the "stone was cut out without hands" symbolizes the physical Jerusalem of their day.[325] These 120 souls are under the "Old Covenant," they came out of Jerusalem, and they will transition from the "Old Covenant" to the "New Covenant." The Holy Spirit "appeared unto them cloven tongues like as of fire, and it sat upon each of them"[326] on the "Day of Pentecost." In the OT, the "Day of Pentecost" is known as the "Feast of Weeks" ordinance. This ordinance, like the others in the OT, points to the future fulfillment of the "Covenant of Redemption," the "Covenant of Promise," and the "Old Covenant" by Jesus.

David Angers the LORD by Counting Israel

The Israelites that enter the "Promise Land" with Joshua and Caleb point to this second group that cannot be numbered, the "New Jerusalem." Consequently, these Israelites are not to be numbered after entering the "Promised Land." The LORD becomes angry at David for ordering "Joab the captain of the host, which was with him, Go now through all the tribes of Israel, from Dan even to Beersheba, and number ye the people, that I may know the number of the people."[327] The key

---

325 Isa. 2:1–3, 66:20; Dan. 9:16; Zec. 8:3
326 Acts 2:3
327 2 Sam. 24:2

point in this story is that David numbered Israel while they are in the "Promised Land."

Joab warned David not to number Israel. He tells him that "the LORD thy God add unto the people, how many soever they be, an hundredfold, and that the eyes of my lord the king may see it: but why doth my lord the king delight in this thing?"[328] Nevertheless, David "prevailed against Joab, and against the captains of the host. And Joab and the captains of the host went out from the presence of the king, to number the people of Israel."[329]

"David's heart smote him after that he had numbered the people. And David said unto the LORD, I have sinned greatly in that I have done: and now, I beseech thee, O LORD, take away the iniquity of thy servant; for I have done very foolishly."[330] Because of David's sin, the LORD, through the prophet Gad, sends David a choice of three punishments: "Seven years of famine come unto thee in thy land? or wilt thou flee three months before thine enemies, while they pursue thee? or that there be three days' pestilence in thy land?"[331] In the end, "the LORD sent a pestilence upon Israel

---

328 2 Sam. 24:3
329 2 Sam. 24:4
330 2 Sam. 24:10
331 2 Sam. 24:13

from the morning even to the time appointed: and there died of the people from Dan even to Beersheba seventy thousand men."[332]

Numbered Twice after the Exodus

The only times that the LORD sanctions the numbering of the Children of Israel are when they are leaving physical or spiritual bondage for a physical or spiritual "Promised Land" and when they are about to enter a physical or spiritual "Promised Land." For example, the Children of Israel were numbered after leaving bondage in the Book of Ezra and in the Book of Acts. They are also numbered again in the Book of Numbers in preparation for entering the "Promised Land."[333]

In Ezra, the Children of Israel are numbered when they depart bondage in Babylon for the "Promised Land." Babylon is a type of Egypt—both physically and spiritually. The Egyptians hold the Children of Israel in physical bondage for 210 years.[334] The Babylonians hold them in physical bondage for seventy years.[335]

---

332 2 Sam. 24:15
333 Num. 26
334 A detailed discussion of the 210 years is in chapter 20
335 2 Chr. 36:17–21, Jer. 25:9–12, Dan. 9:2

In the Book of Acts, on the "Day of Pentecost," "they that gladly received his word were baptized: and the same day there were added unto them about three thousand souls." These 3,000 souls are added to the existing 120 souls recorded in Acts 1:15. All these souls are physical "seed" of Abram and came out of the bondage of the Jewish leadership in Jerusalem.

The Spiritual Bondage of God's People

Jesus says that "the scribes and the Pharisees sit in Moses' seat."[336] He then adds that they hold His people in physical and spiritual bondage by binding "heavy burdens and grievous to be borne, and lay them on men's shoulders; but they themselves will not move them with one of their fingers. But all their works they do for to be seen of men: they make broad their phylacteries, and enlarge the borders of their garments, And love the uppermost rooms at feasts, and the chief seats in the synagogues, And greetings in the markets, and to be called of men, Rabbi, Rabbi."[337] Furthermore, Jesus told them that they "shut up the kingdom of heaven against men: for ye neither go in

---

336 Matt. 23:2
337 Matt. 23:4–7

yourselves, neither suffer ye them that are entering to go in."[338]

The Children of Israel are physically brought out of Egypt, Babylon, and Jerusalem (Jerusalem was a spiritual Egypt).[339] However, the spiritual components of their bondage last far longer than their physical bondage. One may conclude that the Egyptian, Babylonian, Greek, and Roman religious and cultural apostatizing of Judaism and the "Old Covenant" is consolidated in the symbolism of Hagar.

This is because Hagar, an Egyptian handmaid, is given as a gift to Sarai by the Egyptian Pharaoh,[340] and she is included in the substance that Abram brings out of Egypt. Likewise, the Egyptians, Babylonians, Romans, and the Jewish leadership in Jerusalem give God's people gifts. Their gifts, however, are their religions, cultures, and teaching that are contrary to God. Nevertheless, God's people take these gifts with them when they leave.

These gifts from the Egyptians, Babylonians, Romans, and the Jewish leadership have a far more lasting effect on the apostatizing of the "Old

---

338 Matt. 23:13
339 Rev. 11:8
340 Jasher 16:24

Covenant" and Judaism. The apostatizing begins with the exodus from Egypt,[341] but the Jewish leadership uses this apostatized form of the "Old Covenant" and Judaism to bring God's people into bondage. Jesus references them when He says, "I know the blasphemy of them which say they are Jews, and are not, but are the synagogue of Satan."[342]

Thus, this apostatizing leads to there being two groups of people bearing the LORD's name in the world. The first group is the ones like Ishmael, born of the flesh to Abram and Hagar—they are the "Old Covenant" Jews. The second group is like Isaac, born of the spirit to Abraham and Sarah—they are the Christians. These two groups of people claim to bear the LORD's name, but they are in a chronic state of enmity in the Book of Acts. Those that are born of the flesh, the "Old Covenant" Jews, persecute those born of the Spirit, the Christians. Jesus gives His Holy Spirit to the Christians on the "Day of Pentecost."

---

341 Eze. 20:1–9
342 Rev. 2:9

CHAPTER 19

Driving Away the Fowls

The Fowls Came

In verse 11, after Abram prepared the animals and is waiting on the LORD, "Fowls came down upon the carcases, Abram drove them away." These fowls have two meanings. The first is Satan attempting to block the fulfillment of the LORD's promises and the establishment of the covenant. The second is the LORD's punishing those for breaking the covenant after the covenant is established. The first meaning will be discussed now, but the second meaning will be discussed later in chapter 24.

The first meaning is a common challenge for many Christians that are waiting on the LORD. Matthew Henry, in his Commentary on Genesis 15:7–11, says, "A watch must be kept upon our spiritual sacrifices. When vain thoughts, like these fowls, come down upon our sacrifices, we must drive them away, and not suffer them to lodge within us, but attend on God without distraction." Both Abram and Sarai struggle with these thoughts and anxieties symbolized by these fowls, as they wait for the LORD to fulfil His promises to Abram. In particular, they grow impatient waiting for the birth of the Promised Seed.

In chapter 16, Sarai, due to her impatience, gives her maid, Hagar, to Abram so "it may be that [she] may obtain children by her."[343] Abram "hearkened to the voice of Sarai."[344] He "went in unto Hagar, and she conceived: and when she saw that she had conceived, her mistress was despised in her eyes."[345] This action results in the birth of Ishmael,[346] a persecutor of the "Son of Promise," Isaac.[347]

These fowls also seem to typify the continual distractions sent by Satan to devour our spiritual sacrifices and to destroy our ability to fulfill the mission that the LORD assigns us. As seen in

---

343 Gen. 16:2
344 Gen. 16:2
345 Gen. 16:4
346 Gen. 16:5–16
347 Gal. 4:29

"The Parable of the Sower,"[348] the fowls devour the seeds that fell by the way side. Jesus explained that "when any one heareth the word of the kingdom, and understandeth it not, then cometh the wicked one, and catcheth away that which was sown in his heart. This is he which received seed by the way side."[349]

Moses Waited and Waved Off the Fowls

The LORD Orchestrates Scenarios

Satan tries repeatedly to use these fowls to block the LORD from fulfilling His promises to His people. Nevertheless, the LORD orchestrates scenarios that will simultaneously bring Glory to Himself, exalt His people, and frustrate Satan's plans. For example, the LORD told Moses, "Speak unto the children of Israel, that they turn and encamp before Pihahiroth, between Migdol and the sea, over against Baalzephon: before it shall ye encamp by the sea."[350]

The LORD tells Moses that "Pharaoh will say of the children of Israel, They are entangled in the land, the wilderness hath shut them in. And I will harden Pharaoh's heart, that he shall follow after

---

348 Matt. 13:1–9
349 Matt. 13:19
350 Exo. 14:2

them; and I will be honoured upon Pharaoh, and upon all his host; that the Egyptians may know that I am the LORD."³⁵¹ In other words, the LORD tells Moses to place the Israelites in a highly vulnerable position. After that, just wait for the Pharaoh's own evil heart to embolden him into making choices that will give the LORD the opportunity to demonstrate His power over the Pharaoh and the Egyptians in the presence of His people.

Thus, the LORD can use the pure heart of a man to embolden him to make decisions that will be good for himself and for the good of others. And, on the other hand, the LORD can use the evil heart of a man to embolden him to make decisions that will destroy himself, but be for the good of others. Yet, in the end, "we know that all things work together for good to them that love God, to them who are the called according to his purpose."³⁵²

Albert Barnes, in his commentary on James 1:14, says, "The fountain or source of all temptation is in man himself. It is true that external inducements to sin may be placed before him, but they would have no force if there was not something in himself to which they corresponded, and over

---

351 Exo. 14:3–4
352 Rom. 8:28

which they might have power. There must be some 'lust'; some desire; some inclination; something which is unsatisfied now, which is made the foundation of the temptation, and which gives it all its power. If there were no capacity for receiving food, or desire for it, objects placed before us appealing to the appetite could never be made a source of temptation; if there were nothing in the soul which could be regarded as the love of acquisition or possession, gold would furnish no temptation; if there were no sensual propensities, we should be in that quarter above the power of temptation."

Though these Scriptures seem to imply that the Pharaoh has no choice in his actions, in reality, the Pharaoh's own desire to enslave the Children of Israel allows his heart to be emboldened at each opportunity to achieve his internal heart's desires. Thus, the Pharaoh cannot say that he is "tempted of God: for God cannot be tempted with evil, neither tempteth he any man: But every man is tempted, when he is drawn away of his own lust, and enticed."[353] In the end, the LORD is "honoured upon Pharaoh," Moses is exalted, "the LORD overthrew the Egyptians in the midst of

---

353 Jam. 1:13, 14

the sea,"[354] and "the people feared the LORD, and believed the LORD, and his servant Moses."[355]

Waving Off Noise and Waiting On the LORD
Moses, however, waves off the attacks of symbolic fowls. Once the children of Israel learn that the Pharaoh and the Egyptian army are approaching, "The children of Israel lifted up their eyes, and, behold, the Egyptians marched after them; and they were sore afraid: and the children of Israel cried out unto the LORD. And they said unto Moses, Because there were no graves in Egypt, hast thou taken us away to die in the wilderness? wherefore hast thou dealt thus with us, to carry us forth out of Egypt? Is not this the word that we did tell thee in Egypt, saying, Let us alone, that we may serve the Egyptians? For it had been better for us to serve the Egyptians, than that we should die in the wilderness."[356]

Moses waves off these symbolic fowls, and he does not succumb to the complaints and fears of people around him. Instead, Moses tells the children of Israel to "fear ye not, stand still, and see the salvation of the LORD, which he will shew to you to day: for the Egyptians whom ye have seen

---

354 Exo. 14, 27
355 Exo. 14:31
356 Exo. 14:10–12

to day, ye shall see them again no more for ever. The LORD shall fight for you, and ye shall hold your peace."[357] Moses does not allow the fears of some in the crowd to distract or hinder him from accomplishing the LORD's mission.

Moses keeps his mind focused on diligently waiting on the LORD—and so should we. We must keep in mind that there may be times in our life when we have done all that the LORD has told us to do, and all that we can do after that is to "fear ye not, stand still, and see the salvation of the LORD." And, as with Moses, the LORD can simultaneously exalt Himself, exalt you, and destroy a source of evil in your life. However, we must wave off the distractions that Satan sends against us. Satan will try to keep you from carrying out the LORD's mission, and he will try to keep you from receiving the marvelous promises that the LORD has made to you.

David Waited On the LORD

In the First Book of Samuel, "Samuel took the horn of oil, and anointed [David] in the midst of his brethren: and the Spirit of the LORD came upon David from that day forward,"[358] and David

---

357 Exo. 14:13–14
358 1 Sam. 16:13

is anointed King of Israel.[359] However, David is a young lad at the time, the youngest of eight sons born to his father Jesse,[360] and he will not take the throne until he is 30 years old.[361] Thus, David waits several years for the LORD to fulfill His promise to make him King of Israel.

Like with Abram and Moses, David suffers many attacks by symbolic fowls. Most of these attacks come from Saul while waiting on the LORD to make him King of Israel. The LORD uses Saul's attacks on David to fulfill His promise, to exalt Himself, to exalt David, and to simultaneously allow Saul to end his own kingship over Israel by being "drawn away of his own lust, and enticed."[362] Thus, Saul's envy and jealousy were his own undoing.

The Fowls and the Battle of Good versus Evil
In this battle of good versus evil, Satan's evil attacks are meant to not only destroy us directly, but they are also meant to provoke us to return evil for evil and to endanger our relationship with the LORD. Evil tries to put at risk the promises that the LORD made to us and to ultimately cause

---

359 1 Sam. 16:1–13
360 1 Sam. 16:10–11
361 2 Sam. 5:4
362 Jam. 1:14

us to lose our salvation. The evil directed toward us can breed hatred, and hatred can breed sin, and sin can lead to death. We must remember that, in spite of all the attacks from Saul, David did not return evil for evil. "David behaved himself wisely in all his ways; and the LORD was with him. Wherefore when Saul saw that he behaved himself very wisely, he was afraid of him."[363]

Returning Good for Evil
David returns Saul's evil with good. For example, "Saul took three thousand chosen men out of all Israel, and went to seek David and his men upon the rocks of the wild goats. And he came to the sheepcotes by the way, where was a cave; and Saul went in to cover his feet: and David and his men remained in the sides of the cave. And the men of David said unto him, Behold the day of which the LORD said unto thee, Behold, I will deliver thine enemy into thine hand, that thou mayest do to him as it shall seem good unto thee. Then David arose, and cut off the skirt of Saul's robe privily."[364]

David then rebukes his men. He tells them that "the LORD forbid that I should do this thing unto my master, the LORD'S anointed, to stretch forth mine hand against him, seeing he is the anointed

---

363 1 Sam. 18:14, 15
364 1 Sam. 24:2–4

of the LORD. So David stayed his servants with these words, and suffered them not to rise against Saul"[365] and seek revenge; he does not return evil for evil.

Wait On the LORD, Evildoers Are Cut Down
David waits on the LORD. He says, "Fret not thyself because of evildoers, neither be thou envious against the workers of iniquity. For they shall soon be cut down like the grass, and wither as the green herb. Trust in the LORD, and do good; so shalt thou dwell in the land, and verily thou shalt be fed. Delight thyself also in the LORD; and he shall give thee the desires of thine heart. Commit thy way unto the LORD; trust also in him; and he shall bring it to pass. And he shall bring forth thy righteousness as the light, and thy judgment as the noonday."[366]

David instructs us to "rest in the LORD, and wait patiently for him: fret not thyself because of him who prospereth in his way, because of the man who bringeth wicked devices to pass. Cease from anger, and forsake wrath: fret not thyself in any wise to do evil. For evildoers shall be cut off: but

---

365 1 Sam. 24:6, 7
366 Psa. 37:1–6

those that wait upon the LORD, they shall inherit the earth."[367]

---

367 Psa. 37:7–9

CHAPTER 20

Servitude to Great Substance

The LORD Prophesied the Pattern

In verse 12, the LORD gives Abram additional details about the events leading up to his "seed" receiving the carnal "Promised Land." "When the sun was going down, a deep sleep fell upon Abram; and, lo, an horror of great darkness fell upon him. And he said unto Abram, Know of a surety that thy seed shall be a stranger in a land that is not theirs, and shall serve them; and they shall afflict them four hundred years; And also that nation, whom they shall serve, will I judge: and afterward shall they come out with great substance."[368]

---

368 Gen. 15:12–14

The 400-Year Span from Isaac to the Exodus

Though Ishmael's birth is one of the events prophesied in Genesis 15:9–21, the LORD does not use Ishmael's birth to establish the timing of the second prophesied event, nor does He put Ishmael in the lineage of the "Covenant of Promise" or the "Old Covenant." More specifically, the LORD does not place Ishmael in the lineage of the "seed" identified in Genesis 15:13–16. The LORD only uses the birth of Ishmael to point to the birth of a future "seed" of Abram that will be "born after the flesh,"[369] like Ishmael, and born under the "Old Covenant." They will not be Ishmael's carnal "seed," but they will have the nature of Ishmael.

The LORD rejects Ishmael's nature. And, after the birth of Isaac, the LORD supports Sarah's request that Abraham "cast out this bondwoman and [Ishmael]"[370] into the "wilderness." The casting out of Ishmael points to what the LORD does in the "last days" to the future "seed" of Abram that is born under the "Old Covenant" and after the flesh like Ishmael. Because they will reject Jesus, Jesus will reject them and cast them out.

---

369 Gal. 4:23
370 Gen. 21:10

On the other hand, the LORD makes clear that "in Isaac shall [Abraham's] seed be called."[371] Thus, the LORD makes Isaac a "Son of Promise." Thereby, the LORD puts Isaac in the lineage of the "Covenant of Promise," and He puts him in the lineage of the "seed" identified in Genesis 15:13–16.

Consequently, Isaac's birth marks the beginning of the 400 years of Abraham's "seed" being "a stranger in a land that is not theirs, and shall serve them; and they shall afflict them four hundred years; And also that nation, whom they shall serve, will I judge: and afterward shall they come out with great substance."[372] This 400-year span will end at the exodus of the Children of Israel from Egypt.

The Pattern Began with Isaac

Each generation of Abraham's "seed," from the birth of Isaac to the exodus of the Children of Israel from Egypt, will sojourn in a land that is not theirs, they will serve in some type of servitude, they will suffer an increasing level of affliction per generation, and they will consistently exit

---

371 Gen. 21:12
372 Gen. 15:13–14

each event of servitude and affliction with great substance.

The birth of Isaac—which occurs while his father, Abraham, is under the rule of Abimelech[373]—starts the pattern of going into servitude and affliction and then coming out with wealth. Isaac continues this pattern after becoming an adult when he goes back to Gerar and submits to the rule of Abimelech. And, as is prophesied in Genesis 15:14, Isaac comes out with great substance,[374] but no land. As such, the LORD tells Isaac that "unto thee, and unto thy "seed," I will give all these countries."[375] The LORD speaks of a future day for transferring possession of the land. But, for now, Isaac is dwelling in a land that is not his.

The Pattern Continued with Jacob

The pattern is repeated sixty years later[376] with the birth of Jacob, Isaac's son. Jacob serves Laban for "twenty years:"[377] "fourteen years for [his] two daughters, and six years for [his] cattle: and thou hast changed my wages ten times. Except the God of my father, the God of Abraham, and the

---

373 Gen. 21:22–34
374 Gen. 26:1–14
375 Gen. 26:3
376 Gen. 25:26
377 Gen. 31:41

fear of Isaac, had been with me, surely thou hadst sent me away now empty. God hath seen mine affliction and the labour of my hands, and rebuked thee yesternight."[378] Interestingly, Jacob uses two of the same words that the LORD uses in Genesis 15:13: "served" and "afflict."

These words are not used to describe what Isaac goes through under the rule of Abimelech. This is an indication that the oppression of Jacob is greater than the oppression experienced by Isaac. Moreover, this may suggest a pattern of increasing oppression in each generation. Jacob, like his father Isaac and his grandfather Abraham, is not in his own land.

While Jacob is serving Laban, the LORD blesses Jacob, and Jacob "increased exceedingly, and had much cattle, and maidservants, and menservants, and camels, and asses."[379] And, because of this, Jacob comes out from under the servitude and affliction of Laban with great substance.[380]

---

378 Gen. 31:41–42
379 Gen. 30:43
380 Gen. 31:1-9

The Pattern Continued with the Twelve

This pattern of servitude, affliction, and "[coming out] with great substance" is repeated the last time in the next generation, the generation of Jacob's/Israel's twelve sons. Because there is a famine "over all the face of the earth: And Joseph opened all the storehouses, and sold unto the Egyptians; and the famine waxed sore in the land of Egypt. And all countries came into Egypt to Joseph for to buy corn; because that the famine was so sore in all lands."[381] Consequently, "God spake unto Israel in the visions of the night, and said, Jacob, Jacob. And he said, Here am I. And he said, I am God, the God of thy father: fear not to go down into Egypt; for I will there make of thee a great nation: I will go down with thee into Egypt; and I will also surely bring thee up again: and Joseph shall put his hand upon thine eyes."[382] Interestingly, Jacob/Israel is going down to Egypt under God's directions for the same reason that Abram goes down to Egypt in Genesis chapter 12, there is a famine in the land.

At 130 years old,[383] Jacob enters Egypt with his family. "All the souls that came with Jacob into

---

381 Gen. 41:56–57
382 Gen. 46:2–4
383 Gen. 47:9

Egypt, which came out of his loins, besides Jacob's sons' wives, all the souls were threescore and six; And the sons of Joseph, which were born him in Egypt, were two souls: all the souls of the house of Jacob, which came into Egypt, were threescore and ten."[384] However, after dwelling several years in Egypt, "there arose up a new king over Egypt, which knew not Joseph. And he said unto his people, Behold, the people of the children of Israel are more and mightier than we: Come on, let us deal wisely with them; lest they multiply, and it come to pass, that, when there falleth out any war, they join also unto our enemies, and fight against us, and so get them up out of the land. Therefore they did set over them taskmasters to afflict them with their burdens."[385] This will be the last time that Abram's "seeds" will be brought into servitude and affliction before they enter the "Promised Land."

In all, the Children of Israel spend 210 years in Egypt. The 210 years is based on taking the 400-year total, subtracting the 60 years from the birth of Isaac to the birth of Jacob, and subtracting another 130 years from the birth of Jacob to his entry into Egypt. And, after the 210 years, the LORD sends Moses to free them. During their exit

---

384 Gen. 46:26–27
385 Exo. 1:8–11

from Egypt, "the children of Israel did according to the word of Moses; and they borrowed of the Egyptians jewels of silver, and jewels of gold, and raiment: And the LORD gave the people favour in the sight of the Egyptians, so that they lent unto them such things as they required. And they spoiled the Egyptians."[386]

Abram's "seed" that sojourned in Egypt go into servitude and are afflicted. But, just as is prophesied in Genesis 15:14, "they come out with great substance." And, another point that should be made, their oppression is far greater than what Isaac and Jacob experienced—we do not read that Isaac or Jacob are placed under "taskmasters to afflict them with their burdens."

---

386 Exo. 12:35–36

CHAPTER 21

But in the Fourth Generation

In Genesis 15:15–16, the LORD tells Abram that he "shalt go to thy fathers in peace; thou shalt be buried in a good old age. But in the fourth generation they shall come hither again: for the iniquity of the Amorites is not yet full."[387] Because the phrase "in the fourth generation" comes after the LORD tells Abram that he "shalt be buried in a good old age," the fourth generation should be counted from Abraham's death. This is because Abram and Abraham share the same body, but not the same role. The LORD identifies that a difference in their roles exists by the name change.

The Bible reads that "the days of the years of Abraham's life which he lived, an hundred

---

387 Gen. 15:15–16

threescore and fifteen years,"[388] and Jacob is 15 years old when Abraham dies.[389] Hence, Abraham dies in the generation of Jacob, and he does not see the generation of Jacob's children. Therefore, the first of the four generations is the generation of Jacob's children, in particular Levi, and it ends with Moses. Choosing the count to begin with the generation of Levi, and not the other eleven male children of Jacob, is because: (1) the LORD uses Moses, a descendant of Levi, to deliver the Children of Israel out of Egypt; and, (2) the lifespans of the descendants of the other eleven male children of Jacob/Israel are not mentioned.[390]

The only other male children of Jacob considered as starting points are Judah and Joseph. The reason for Judah is the "Son of Promise" is in his lineage. The reason for Joseph is Joshua is in his lineage.[391] The Bible, however, only gives information on the lifespan and lineage of Levi.

---

388 Gen. 25:7

389 Abraham was 100 when Isaac was born (Gen. 21:5), and Isaac was 60 when Jacob was born. Thus, Jacob was 15 when Abraham died (175–100–60=15)

390 Exo. 6:16–20

391 Num. 13:8, 16

CHAPTER 22

Other Related Timespans

Exodus 6:16–20

In Exodus 6:16–20, the lineage of Levi to Moses is given. "The names of the sons of Levi according to their generations; Gershon, and Kohath, and Merari: and the years of the life of Levi were an hundred thirty and seven years. The sons of Gershon; Libni, and Shimi, according to their families. And the sons of Kohath; Amram, and Izhar, and Hebron, and Uzziel: and the years of the life of Kohath were an hundred thirty and three years. And the sons of Merari; Mahali and Mushi: these are the families of Levi according to their generations. And Amram took him Jochebed his father's sister to wife; and she bare him Aaron and Moses:

and the years of the life of Amram were an hundred and thirty and seven years."[392]

By adding the lifespans of Levi (137), Kohath (133), Amram (137), and Moses' age at the exodus,[393] we get 487 years. And, considering the inevitable overlap of lifespans, the 487 years fit within the 400-year window in Genesis 15:13. However, Kohath is born prior to his entry into Egypt.[394] Thus, the earliest that the 400 years could start, if the entire 400 years are spent in Egypt, is near the birth of Kohath. Consequently, the combined lifespans of Kohath and Amram are 270 years, leaving a minimum gap of fifty years between the death of Amram, Moses' father, and the birth of Moses. The concept that the 400 years is spent in Egypt means Moses is born no less than fifty years after his father dies. This scenario is not possible.

Exodus 12:40–41

Exodus 12:40–41 reads that "now the sojourning of the children of Israel, who dwelt in Egypt, was four hundred and thirty years. And it came to pass at the end of the four hundred and thirty

---

392 Exo. 6:16–20
393 Exo. 7:7
394 Gen. 46:8–11

years, even the selfsame day it came to pass, that all the hosts of the LORD went out from the land of Egypt."

Exodus 12:40 suggests that the 430 years begin either with the children of Israel, with their entry into Egypt, or when they are placed, by the Pharaoh, into bondage. If it begins with the children of Israel, the earliest that it could possibly begin is at the birth of Reuben, the firstborn. This is about fifty years before they enter Egypt.[395] Hence, 380 years are left for their stay in Egypt.

By subtracting Moses' age at the exodus (eighty years) from the 380, we are left with 300 years for Kohath to father Amram and for Amram to father Moses. This corresponds to a 150-year average age for Kohath to father Amram and for Amram to father Moses. This is not possible because Kohath and Amram lived 133 and 137 years, respectively. Thus, the 430 years cannot begin with Reuben, or later.

If we assume that the 430 years begin at entry into Egypt, and we subtract Moses' age at the exodus, we get 350 years for Kohath to father Amram and for Amram to father Kohath—an average age at

---

395 Jasher 62:1

conception of 175 years. This explanation is even more implausible.

The Treasury of Scripture Knowledge (TSK) commentary explains this apparent inconsistency in Exodus 12:40–41. The TSK identifies an issue in the manuscript translated by the KJV.

The Samaritan Pentateuch reads, "Now the sojourning of the children of Israel, and of their fathers in the land of Canaan and in the land of Egypt, was 430 years." The Alexandrine copy of the LXX has the same reading; and the same statement is made by the apostle Paul, in Gal. 3:17, who reckons from the promise made to Abraham to the giving of the law. That these three witnesses have the truth, the chronology itself proves; for it is evident that the descendants of Israel did not dwell 430 years in Egypt; while it is equally evident, that the period from Abraham's entry into Canaan to the Exodus, is exactly that number. Thus, from Abraham's entrance into the promised land to the birth of Isaac, was 25 years; Isaac was 60 at the birth of Jacob; Jacob was 130 at his going into Egypt; where he and his children continued 215 years more; making in the whole 430 years. See Kennicott's Dissertation on the Hebrew Text.

According to the TSK, the Samaritan Pentateuch and the Alexandrine copy of the LXX records Exodus 12:40–41 include the phrase "and of their fathers." This phrase allows the inclusion of Abraham and Isaac in the 430 years, the 400-year prophesy in Genesis chapter 15 to begin at the birth of Isaac, and the 430 years to begin at the confirmation of the covenant with Abraham.[396] This is more consistent with the Scriptures in the Bible: Galatians 3:17, 1 Kings 6:1, and Acts 13:17–22.

Galatians 3:17

In Galatian 3:17, Paul states "that the covenant, that was confirmed before of God in Christ, the law, which was four hundred and thirty years after, cannot disannul, that it should make the promise of none effect." Paul is referring to the "Covenant of Promise" that God confirms with Abraham 430 years before the establishment of the "Old Covenant" at Mount Sinai. Thus, the 400 years begin with Isaac, but the 430 years do not begin with Isaac. This is because the confirming of the "Covenant of Promise" occurs prior to the birth of Isaac. Thus, the 430 years include the 400 years in Genesis 15:13.

---

396 Gal. 3:17

To understand the 430 years, we must go to the Book of Acts in the Bible and to the Book of Jasher.[397] In the Book of Acts, Stephen reiterates that the first calling of Abram by the LORD comes before Genesis chapter 12. Stephen says that "the God of glory appeared unto our father Abraham, when he was in Mesopotamia, before he dwelt in Charran, And said unto him, Get thee out of thy country, and from thy kindred, and come into the land which I shall shew thee."[398] This happens years before Genesis chapter 12.

There is also language in the Book of Jasher that leads to this same conclusion. In Jasher chapter 12, Abram says, "Let us arise and go to the land of Canaan, out of the reach of injury from Nimrod; and serve thou the Lord who created thee in the earth and it will be well with thee; and cast away all the vain things which thou pursuest. And Abram ceased to speak, when Noah and his son Shem answered Terah, saying, True is the word which Abram hath said unto thee. And Terah hearkened to the voice of his son Abram, and Terah did all that Abram said, for this was from the Lord, that

---

[397] The Book of Jasher, Referred to in Joshua and Second Samuel; Faithfully Tr. from the Original Hebrew into English. Published by J.H. Parry & Co, 1887.
[398] Acts 7:2–3

the king should not cause Abram's death."³⁹⁹ Thus, Stephen and the Book of Jasher both state that the LORD calls Abram, and Abram tells Terah to depart for the land of Canaan. This happens when Abram is about fifty-two years old.⁴⁰⁰

After Abram leaves Ur of the Chaldees and spends three years in Haran, we read in the Book of Jasher chapter 13 that the Lord appears to Abram and tells him: "I am the Lord who brought thee forth from Ur Casdim, and delivered thee from the hands of all thine enemies. And now therefore if thou wilt hearken to my voice and keep my commandments, my statutes and my laws, then will I cause thy enemies to fall before thee, and I will multiply thy seed like the stars of heaven, and I will send my blessing upon all the works of thy hands, and thou shalt lack nothing. Arise now, take thy wife and all belonging to thee and go to the land of Canaan and remain there, and I will there be unto thee for a God, and I will bless thee. And Abram rose and took his wife and all belonging to him, and he went to the land of Canaan as the Lord had told him; and Abram was fifty [and five] years old when he went from Haran."⁴⁰¹

---

399 Jasher 12:68–70
400 Jasher 12:57
401 Jasher 13:3–5, (Though Jasher 13:5 reads that Abram was 50 years old when he went to Canaan, Jasher 12:9, 12:45,

However, "Nahor, Abram's brother, and Terah his father, and Lot the son of Haran and all belonging to them dwelt in Haran,"[402] they do not go with Abram.

Later, "In the fifteenth year of Abram's dwelling in the land of Canaan, which is the seventieth year of the life of Abram, and the Lord appeared to Abram in that year and he said to him, I am the Lord who brought thee out from Ur Casdim to give thee this land for an inheritance. Now therefore walk before me and be perfect and keep my commands, for to thee and to thy seed I will give this land for an inheritance, from the river Mitzraim unto the great river Euphrates. And thou shalt come to thy fathers in peace and in good age, and the fourth generation shall return here in this land and shall inherit it forever; and Abram built an altar, and he called upon the name of the Lord who appeared to him, and he brought up sacrifices upon the altar to the Lord. At that time Abram returned and went to Haran to see his father and mother, and his father's household, and Abram and his wife and all belonging to him returned to Haran, and Abram dwelt in Haran five years."[403]

12:57, 13:3, 13:9, and 13:17 all strongly suggest that Abram was 55 years old when he went to Canaan.)
402 Jasher 13:10
403 Jasher 13:17–20

The language in the Book of Jasher chapter 13 reads very similarly to the language in Genesis chapter 15. This event in Jasher chapter 13, when Abram is 70 years old, probably marks the confirmation of the covenant spoken of by Paul in Galatians 3:15–17. Therefore, the 430 years begin when Abram is 70 years old. And, after spending five more years in Haran, Abram is 75 years old when the Bible picks up with his calling in Genesis 12:1. However, after this calling in Genesis chapter 12, Abram brings Lot with him.

1 Kings 6:1 and Acts 13:17–21

In 1 King 6:1, we read, "And it came to pass in the four hundred and eightieth year after the children of Israel were come out of the land of Egypt, in the fourth year of Solomon's reign over Israel, in the month Zif, which is the second month, that he began to build the house of the LORD."[404]

These 480 years include a large portion of the history that Paul reviews in Acts chapter 13. Paul states that "the God of this people of Israel chose our fathers, and exalted the people when they dwelt as strangers in the land of Egypt, and with an high arm brought he them out of it And about

---

404 1 Kin. 6:1

the time of forty years suffered he their manners in the wilderness."[405]

Paul adds that "when he had destroyed seven nations in the land of Chanaan, he divided their land to them by lot. And after that he gave unto them judges about the space of four hundred and fifty years, until Samuel the prophet. And afterward they desired a king: and God gave unto them Saul the son of Cis, a man of the tribe of Benjamin, by the space of forty years."[406]

Thus, the 480 years does not include the years that the Children of Israel spent in Egypt, but it does include the years between the exodus to Saul the King. The 450 years, however, begin when the Egyptians begin afflicting and enslaving the children of Israel. This is 101 years after the children of Israel entered Egypt and after the last son of Jacob dies, which is Levi.[407] Moreover, the 450 years identified in Acts 13:20 is 109 years before the beginning of the 480 years identified in 1 Kings 6:1.

---

405 Acts 13:17, 18
406 Acts 13:19–21
407 Jasher 63:1

CHAPTER 23

The Amorites' Iniquity Not Yet Full

The Three Salient Points

In the last clause of verse 16, the LORD states the reason for the delay in giving Abram's seed the "Promised Land" is because "the iniquity of the Amorites is not yet full."[408] This clause contains three salient points. First, the timeline for Abram's seed receiving the "Promised Land" is driven by the Amorites. Second, Abram's "seeds" will be the LORD's instrument to bring judgment against the Amorites. Third, a timeline is given for when the LORD's patience and long-suffering would run out.

---

408 Gen. 15:16

Thus, there is a point when the LORD no longer hears our prayers. In the Book of Isaiah, the LORD said, "Seek ye the LORD while he may be found, call ye upon him while he is near."[409] Moreover, Jesus warned that "once the master of the house is risen up, and hath shut to the door, and ye begin to stand without, and to knock at the door, saying, Lord, Lord, open unto us; and he shall answer and say unto you, I know you not whence ye are."[410]

The Timeline for the Promised Land

Salient Point One: The "Promised Land" delivered to Abram's "seed" is not based entirely on their behavior or achievements. Instead, it is also determined by the behavior and the long-suffering that the LORD will show another nation, the Amorites. We often believe that the LORD's timeline for fulfilling His promises is totally dependent on our behavior. But, in reality, there may be other factors that may be unknown to us. In this case, the LORD tells Abram that the timeline for his seed to receive the "Promised Land" is based on the behavior of the Amorites.

We should realize that, while the LORD is working His promises for us, He is simultaneously working His promises for others and fulfilling

---

409 Isa. 55:6
410 Luk. 13:25

them in a time frame that meets the needs of all His people. Consequently, sometimes, while the LORD is working His will for us, all we can do is what David said, "Wait on the LORD, and keep his way, and he shall exalt thee to inherit the land."[411]

Abram's Seed, An Instrument for Judgment
Salient Point Two: The LORD will use Abram's seed to bring judgment upon the Amorites.[412] This prophesied event marks a change in how the LORD will bring ultimate-carnal judgment upon nations. Before the destruction of the Amorites, the LORD uses His "might and power"[413] to send a flood to destroy the world in the days of Noah, sends "brimstone and fire"[414] to destroy Sodom and Gomorrah, and uses seawater to destroy the Egyptians. However, beginning with the Amorites, the LORD begins using His "spirit"[415] to "stir up"[416] specific nations to execute His ultimate-carnal judgment on another nation.

---

411 Psa. 37: 34
412 "What Does Genesis 15:16 Mean?" BibleRef.com. Accessed April 24, 2022. https://www.bibleref.com/Genesis/15/Genesis-15-16.html.
413 Zec. 4:6
414 Gen. 19:24
415 Zec. 4:6, Isa. 13:17–22, the Book of Habakkuk
416 Isa. 5:8–30, 13:17, 44:28–45-1; Dan. 7:1–10, 11:2

The LORD does this with the Babylonians, Persians, Greeks, and Romans.[417] This is symbolized when Daniel "saw in [his] vision by night, and, behold, the four winds of the heaven strove upon the great sea. And four great beasts came up from the sea, diverse one from another." In Daniel's vision, recorded in Daniel 7:1-3, the "sea" represents the gentile world, the "beasts" represents four nations, and the "winds" represent the "Spirit" of the LORD stirring up these four nations.

A Timeline for Judgment
Salient Point Three: The LORD gives a timeline for when His patience and long-suffering will end for the Amorites. Yet, the timeline that is given Abram is still not clearly defined. This is because Abram does not know when Isaac will be born.

The next time a timeline is given to a man for a nation is in the "70-week" prophecy in the Book of Daniel. In this prophecy, the LORD tells Daniel that His patience and long-suffering for His people, the Israelites, will end "70 weeks" (70 times 7, or 490 years) "from the going forth of the commandment to restore and to build Jerusalem."[418]

---

417 The Book of Habakkuk
418 Dan. 9:25

Comparison to Daniel's "70-Week" Prophecy

This prophecy in Genesis chapter 15 is similar to the "70-week" prophecy in Daniel chapter 9. Both prophecies depict the LORD telling a man that His patience and long-suffering for a nation will end in a specific year. Each has a starting date that is based on a future event. And both prophecies come to fruition.

The "70-week" prophecy's starting point is "the going forth of the commandment to restore and to build Jerusalem." This happens in 457 BC,[419] And, since the prophecy is given to Daniel around 540 BC,[420] he does not know when the prophecy will begin. Similarly, Abram does not know when the 400 years will begin because he does not know when Isaac will be born.

The second similarity is that both prophecies are directed at nations that are behaving contrary to the LORD's will, and the LORD establishes a deadline for them to repent. In the Book of Daniel's "70-week" prophecy, the nation is Israel. In the 400-year prophecy in the Book of Genesis, the nation is the Amorites.

---

419 Based on the decree in Ezra 7
420 This is based on the prophecy being given in the first year of Darius, the son of Ahasuerus (Dan. 9:1)

The third similarity is that neither nation changes their behavior for the good. Thus, the LORD uses His "spirit" to "stir up" another nation to execute His judgment and to fulfill His prophecy. The fulfillment of the prophecy concerning the Amorites is written in Joshua chapter 10. We read that "the five kings of the Amorites, the king of Jerusalem, the king of Hebron, the king of Jarmuth, the king of Lachish, the king of Eglon, gathered themselves together, and went up, they and all their hosts, and encamped before Gibeon, and made war against it. And the men of Gibeon sent unto Joshua to the camp to Gilgal, saying, Slack not thy hand from thy servants; come up to us quickly, and save us, and help us: for all the kings of the Amorites that dwell in the mountains are gathered together against us. So Joshua ascended from Gilgal, he, and all the people of war with him, and all the mighty men of valour. And the LORD said unto Joshua, Fear them not: for I have delivered them into thine hand; there shall not a man of them stand before thee."[421]

In verses 9–11, we read, "Joshua therefore came unto them suddenly, and went up from Gilgal all night. And the LORD discomfited them before Israel, and slew them with a great slaughter at Gibeon, and chased them along the way that goeth

---

421 Jos. 10:5–8

up to Bethhoron, and smote them to Azekah, and unto Makkedah. And it came to pass, as they fled from before Israel, and were in the going down to Bethhoron, that the LORD cast down great stones from heaven upon them unto Azekah, and they died: they were more which died with hailstones than they whom the children of Israel slew with the sword."[422]

Afterward, "Spake Joshua to the LORD in the day when the LORD delivered up the Amorites before the children of Israel, and he said in the sight of Israel, Sun, stand thou still upon Gibeon; and thou, Moon, in the valley of Ajalon. And the sun stood still, and the moon stayed, until the people had avenged themselves upon their enemies. Is not this written in the book of Jasher? So the sun stood still in the midst of heaven, and hasted not to go down about a whole day. And there was no day like that before it or after it, that the LORD hearkened unto the voice of a man: for the LORD fought for Israel."[423]

And lastly, we read that "five kings fled, and hid themselves in a cave at Makkedah. And it was told Joshua, saying, The five kings are found hid in a cave at Makkedah. And Joshua said, Roll great

---

422 Jos. 10:9–11
423 Jos. 10:12–14

stones upon the mouth of the cave, and set men by it for to keep them: And stay ye not, but pursue after your enemies, and smite the hindmost of them; suffer them not to enter into their cities: for the LORD your God hath delivered them into your hand. And it came to pass, when Joshua and the children of Israel had made an end of slaying them with a very great slaughter, till they were consumed, that the rest which remained of them entered into fenced cities."[424]

The fulfillment of the "70-week" prophecy is not recorded in the Bible. However, Jesus prophesied the destruction of the temple in AD 70. Jesus said, in referring to the Temple in Jerusalem, "See ye not all these things? verily I say unto you, There shall not be left here one stone upon another, that shall not be thrown down."[425] This is fulfilled in AD 70 when Jesus sends the Romans to destroy and burn the Temple and Jerusalem. This historical event marked the "end of the world" for the Nation of Israel and the "Old Covenant." And, just as the LORD did with regard to "The Flood,"[426] Sodom and Gomorrah, and the first destruction

---

424 Jos. 10: 16–20
425 Matt. 24:2
426 1 Pet. 3:20

of Jerusalem,[427] God sends His angels to retrieve and save His faithful remnant.

For example, in preparing for the first destruction of Jerusalem in 588 BC, God spends the sixteen years between the first deportation and the siege of Jerusalem by Babylon retrieving and evacuating His remnant from Jerusalem.[428] This is done to save them from the coming destruction.[429] In the case of the second destruction of Jerusalem in AD 70, the LORD uses the persecution of the Christians living in Jerusalem by the "Old Covenant" Jews to bring about a separation between these two groups, to bring about an exodus of Christians from Jerusalem, and to bring about a spreading of the Gospel throughout the world after the stoning of Stephen.[430]

The "Old Covenant" Jews' persecution begins with the stoning of Stephen[431] in AD 33. Moreover, the stoning of Stephen marks the end of the "70-weeks" time period but not the fulfillment of prophecy. A reason for saying this is that the stoning of Stephen occurs 490 years after the year 457 BC. Thus, the end of the LORD's patience and

---

427 Jer. 24:1–10
428 Dan. 1:1–2, 2 Kin. 24:10–17
429 Jer. 24:1–10
430 Acts 8:1–4
431 Acts 7:54–60, 11:19

long-suffering with the "Old Covenant" Jews is marked by the stoning of Stephen.

The LORD also brings about individual separations in the OT to save His people. The LORD causes the separation of Ishmael from Isaac to save Isaac. He causes the separation of Esau from Jacob to save Jacob. He also causes the separation of Daniel, Ezekiel, and the Hebrew boys to save them from the destruction of Jerusalem in 588 BC.

Chapter 24

Cutting the Blood Covenant

The Smoking Furnace and the Burning Lamp

Verse 17 reads, "It came to pass, that, when the sun went down, and it was dark, behold a smoking furnace, and a burning lamp that passed between those pieces."[432] Verses 7 thru 16 point to the cutting of this "blood covenant" and lead to the identification of the "smoking furnace" as "God the Father" and the "burning lamp" as "God the Son," Jesus. The identification of the "burning lamp" representing "God the Son" is also supported by other Scriptures that refer to "a lamp" as a son that is born, or will be born, to succeed the father.[433]

---

432 Gen. 15:17
433 Adam Clark Commentary on 1 Kin. 11:36, 15:4; 2 Kin. 8:19; 2 Chr. 21:7

"God the Father" and Jesus Are at Mount Sinai

"God the Father" and Jesus are present at Mount Sinai during the establishment of the "Old Covenant." "God the Father" "spake unto [them] out of the midst of the fire: [they] heard the voice of the words, but saw no similitude; only [they] heard a voice."[434] Furthermore, "Moses, and Aaron, Nadab, and Abihu, and seventy of the elders of Israel"[435] see Jesus. However, Jesus does not speak.

Only "God the Father" speaks the Commandments from Mount Sinai,[436] and He is the One that Moses asks in Exodus chapter 33 to "shew me thy glory."[437] In both cases, no one, not even Moses, sees "God the Father." Moses, speaking about what happened at Mount Sinai, says, "Ye saw no manner of similitude on the day that the LORD spake unto you in Horeb out of the midst of the fire: Lest ye corrupt yourselves, and make you a graven image, the similitude of any figure, the likeness of male or female."[438]

---

434 Deu. 4:12
435 Exo. 24: 9–11
436 Exo. 20-23
437 Exo. 33:18
438 Deu. 4:15–16

Moreover, when Moses asks "God the Father" to "shew me thy glory," He answers, "Thou canst not see my face: for there shall no man see me, and live."[439] Thus, "No man hath seen God at any time."[440] "God the Father" only reveals Himself to man through His Son, Jesus, Who is "the brightness of his glory, and the express image of his person."[441]

Consequently, if the Son is the express image of the Father, He is not the Father. Jesus is the Second Person of the Trinity at Mount Sinai, He is the "God of Israel"[442] seen by "Moses, and Aaron, Nadab, and Abihu, and seventy of the elders of Israel,"[443] and He is seen by Abram in his vision in Genesis 15:1. We also find an NT reference to Jesus being the "God of Israel" in the Book of John, chapter 20. In this chapter, Jesus tells Thomas to, "reach hither thy finger, and behold my hands; and reach hither thy hand, and thrust it into my side: and be not faithless, but believing. And Thomas answered and said unto him, My Lord and my God."[444] Thus, Thomas calls Jesus his God.

---

439 Exo. 33:20
440 Jhn. 1:18
441 Heb. 1:3
442 Exo. 24:10
443 Exo. 24:9
444 Jhn. 20: 27–28

One Speaks, Not Seen. One Seen, Not Heard

Also, the phenomenon at Mount Sinai is similar to what happens in the NT at Jesus' baptism and transfiguration. Before His baptism, Jesus explains to John the Baptist that He must be baptized by him. He tells him, "Suffer it to be so now: for thus it becometh us to fulfil all righteousness." But, immediately after His baptism, "God the Father" speaks from "heaven, saying, this is my beloved Son, in whom I am well pleased."[445] "God the Father" speaks, but He is not seen. Conversely, Jesus is seen, but He is not recorded speaking.

Moreover, when Jesus is "transfigured before them: and his face did shine as the sun, and his raiment was white as the light. And, behold, there appeared unto them Moses and Elias talking with him. Then answered Peter, and said unto Jesus, Lord, it is good for us to be here: if thou wilt, let us make here three tabernacles; one for thee, and one for Moses, and one for Elias. While he yet spake, behold, a bright cloud overshadowed them: and behold a voice out of the cloud, which said, This is my beloved Son, in whom I am well pleased; hear ye him."[446] And, just as with what happens at Mount Sinai and the Baptism of Jesus,

---

445 Matt. 3:17
446 Matt. 17:2–5

God the Father speaks, but He is not seen. Jesus is seen, but He is not heard.

A potential lesson from the aforementioned is that when "God the Father" is speaking, "God the Son" is silent and listening. This lesson applies to us; when someone senior to us is speaking, we should remain silent and listen. Thus, when our parents are speaking, we should remain silent and listen. When our boss is speaking, we should remain silent and listen. And, when the Word of God is being taught and preached, we should remain silent and listen—except in Bible studies and Sunday schools when pertinent questions and input are encouraged.

The Fowls after Cutting the Blood Covenant

We will now discuss the symbolism of the fowls that come down upon carcasses after the cutting of a "blood covenant." This is important because the fowls coming down upon carcasses after the cutting of the "blood covenant" symbolize the LORD's punishment for those who break "blood covenants" with the LORD.

According to "A Smoking Fire Pot," an article published by Ligonier Ministries, the "blood covenant" that the LORD makes with Abram has rites that "[accompany] the agreement in order to signify what would happen if one or both parties failed to live up to their end of the pact. One common ritual involved dismembering animals and then laying the pieces in two [columns] side-by-side with a path in between. The individuals making the covenant would then pass between the animals and invoke a curse upon themselves if they broke the agreement. In performing this rite, both parties were in effect saying, 'If I do not fulfill the terms of this covenant, may the destruction that befell these animals also be upon my head.'"[447]

The penalty for breaking this type of "blood covenant" is illustrated in Jeremiah chapter 34 when "king Zedekiah had made a covenant with all the people which were at Jerusalem, to proclaim liberty unto them; That every man should let his manservant, and every man his maidservant, being an Hebrew or an Hebrewess, go free; that none should serve himself of them, to wit, of a Jew his brother. Now when all the princes, and all the people, which had entered into the covenant, heard that every one should let his manservant, and every one his maidservant, go free, that none

---

[447] "A Smoking Fire Pot: Reformed Bible Studies & Devotionals at Ligonier.org." Ligonier Ministries. Accessed April 24, 2022. https://www.ligonier.org/learn/devotionals/smoking-fire-pot/.

should serve themselves of them any more, then they obeyed, and let them go."[448]

"But afterward they turned, and caused the servants and the handmaids, whom they had let go free, to return, and brought them into subjection for servants and for handmaids."[449] They broke the covenant, and the LORD tells "the men that have transgressed my covenant, which have not performed the words of the covenant which they had made before me, when they cut the calf in twain, and passed between the parts thereof, The princes of Judah, and the princes of Jerusalem, the eunuchs, and the priests, and all the people of the land, which passed between the parts of the calf; I will even give them into the hand of their enemies, and into the hand of them that seek their life: and their dead bodies shall be for meat unto the fowls of the heaven, and to the beasts of the earth."[450]

Thus, the LORD makes them pay the penalty identified in the covenant. This penalty is death, and "their dead bodies shall be for meat unto the fowls of the heaven, and to the beasts of the earth."[451]

---

448 Jer. 34:8–10
449 Jer. 34:11
450 Jer. 34:18–20
451 Jer. 34:20

This phrase refers to the symbolism of the fowls coming down upon carcasses after the cutting of the "blood covenant" and the penalty for breaking the covenant.

A Three-Party "Blood Covenant"

The general terms of the "blood covenant" are identified in Genesis 15:13–16. The "blood covenant," however, is not cut until Genesis 15:17–18 when "God the Father" and Jesus passed through the pieces stating what they are agreeing to do as part of this covenant with Abram.

This is dramatized by the "smoking furnace" and the "burning lamp" passing between the pieces, and the LORD stating, as He passes through the pieces, that He "made a covenant with Abram, saying, Unto thy seed have I given this land, from the river of Egypt unto the great river, the river Euphrates: The Kenites, and the Kenezzites, and the Kadmonites, And the Hittites, and the Perizzites, and the Rephaims, And the Amorites, and the Canaanites, and the Girgashites, and the Jebusites."[452]

And since Abram does not pass through the pieces, no penalty fell upon him. Instead, the penalty

---

452 Gen. 15:18–21

for any party breaking the covenant fell upon either "God the Father" or Jesus. We know as far back as the Garden of Eden that Jesus agrees to pay this penalty. Jesus, JEHOVAH, agrees to pay the penalty for us because "he was manifested to take away our sins; and in him is no sin."[453] Moreover, in 1 John, we read that the "devil sinneth from the beginning, For this purpose the Son of God was manifested, that he might destroy the works of the devil."[454]

Consequently, Jesus assumes the responsibility for paying the penalty. He was sent by "God the Father" to be the substitutional sacrifice for the sins of man in breaking His "blood covenant." Thus, the "blood covenant" that is cut in Genesis chapter 15 is a three-way covenant with the covenanters being "God the Father," Jesus, and Abram.

We find substantiation that this is a three-party covenant when "God the Father" tells Abraham that, He "will establish [His] covenant between me and thee and thy seed after thee in their generations for an everlasting covenant, to be a God unto thee, and to thy seed after thee."[455] Paul explains this verse by saying, "Now to Abraham and

---

453 1 Jhn. 3:5
454 1 Jhn. 3:8
455 Gen. 17:7

his seed were the promises made. He saith not, And to seeds, as of many; but as of one, And to thy seed, which is Christ."[456]

Therefore, this three-party covenant with Abram is a continuation of the "Covenant of Redemption." The "Covenant of Redemption" is like the primary covenant or contract. Afterward, there are subcovenants established in support the "Covenant of Redemption." None of the subcovenants make the "Covenant of Redemption" void, or changes its goals and purpose—they neither modify nor replace. Paul makes a similar observation when he says "that the covenant, that was confirmed before of God in Christ, the law, which was four hundred and thirty years after, cannot disannul, that it should make the promise of none effect."[457] His observation, though it specifically addresses the "Covenant of Promise" and the "Old Covenant," is generally applicable.

Thus, the "Covenant of Promise" that "God the Father" and Jesus make with Abram is nothing more than a subcovenant made in support of the "Covenant of Redemption." The "Covenant of Promise" is not an independent covenant. Moreover, the "Covenant of Promise" makes

---

456 Gal. 3:16
457 Gal. 3:17

clear that Jesus, the redeemer of the "Covenant of Redemption," will come through Noah's son Shem. We know this because Abram comes through the lineage of Shem, and Jesus will come through the lineage of Abraham—beginning with Isaac. And, until this point, the Bible does not state which one of Noah's sons the lineage of Jesus will come through: Shem, Ham, or Japheth.

CHAPTER 25

The Promised Land Boundaries

In verses 18–21, the LORD defines the boundaries of the "Promised Land." The boundaries are "from the river of Egypt unto the great river, the river Euphrates: The Kenites, and the Kenizzites, and the Kadmonites, And the Hittites, and the Perizzites, and the Rephaims, And the Amorites, and the Canaanites, and the Girgashites, and the Jebusites."[458] However, Abram's "seed" never dwelt in the "Promised Land" as defined in Genesis 15:18–21.

They did have rule over a very large portion of the land during the reign of David.[459] But the LORD gives them the land as an exclusive dwelling place. Their failure to take possession of the land and to

---

458 Gen. 15:18–21
459 2 Chr. 9:26

dwell in the land exclusively is due to their disobedience. Moses warns them that "if thine heart turn away, so that thou wilt not hear, but shalt be drawn away, and worship other gods, and serve them; I denounce unto you this day, that ye shall surely perish, and that ye shall not prolong your days upon the land, whither thou passest over Jordan to go to possess it."[460]

---

460 Deu. 30:17–18

CHAPTER 26

Summary

There are at least four "take-a-ways" from Genesis chapter 15. **First**, Jesus is the LORD, JEHOVAH, that appears to Abram in a vision in Genesis chapter 15. Jesus appears to Abram as a Comforter, Protector, and an exceedingly great Reward. He is there when Abram needs him, and He will be there for us when we need Him.

Moreover, Jesus manifests Himself in bodily form to Abraham and Sarah in the plains of Mamre.[461] The Scripture reads that "the LORD (JEHOVAH) appeared unto [Abraham] in the plains of Mamre,"[462] and Jesus is the only Person in the Trinity "that was manifest in the flesh, justified

---
461 Gen. 18:1–15
462 Gen. 18:1

in the Spirit, seen of angels, preached unto the Gentiles, believed on in the world, received up into glory."[463] No other Person in the Trinity manifested Himself in the flesh.

Second, faith is not a lack of anxiety while performing God's mission—anxiety is a natural part of the human nature that God gave us. No, faith is the demonstration of obedience and perseverance in spite of our anxieties. Our obedience and perseverance serve as evidence that we know, understand, and believe "what" the LORD promises us while not knowing and understanding "how" He will protect us and fulfill His promises to us.

Third, we must wave off the fowls sent by Satan to devour our spiritual sacrifices and to destroy our ability to fulfill the LORD's mission. These fowls may also be evil attacks that are meant to not only destroy us directly, but to provoke us to return evil for evil and endanger our relationship with the LORD.

Ultimately, Satan is trying to use us to attack the LORD. He wants to use the LORD's love for us as a weapon against the LORD. We are merely tools for Satan in his battle against the LORD. Satan wants us to work against our own best interest

---

463 1 Tim. 3:16

by deceiving us into putting at risk the awesome promises that the LORD made to us, and to cause us to lose our salvation. We cannot let the evil that Satan directs against us through others breed hatred within us. This hatred can then breed sin, and sin can then lead to spiritual death, and spiritual death is eternal separation from the LORD.

Fourth, the Bible is neither two books, the Old and the New, nor is it a series of sixty-six independent books. Each book is dependent on the other: the OT foretells, and the NT fulfills. Thus, the Bible is one book, with one inspiring author, with several men writing under the inspiration of this author, who is the LORD. Moreover, the Bible tells and retells one cohesive and consistent story, and it provides greater details at each retelling.

This one story is about why Jesus came, how we know that He came, and what we should expect from Jesus, His Father, and the Holy Spirit in eternity. We are to feel confident in who Jesus is and what He did. This is because the OT tells us what He would do, the NT tells us what He did, and they both agree.

Lastly, Jesus tells His followers what will shortly happen to them. He says, "And now I have told you before it come to pass, that, when it is come to pass, ye might believe."[464] Likewise, a goal of this book is to explain Genesis chapter 15 in such a way that the reader will see both the prophecy in Genesis chapter 15 and the fulfillment in the NT. And, as a result, the reader might believe that Jesus is the "Son of God" and leave with a better understanding of the inerrancy of God's Word, the relationship between the OT and the NT, and will either establish or strengthen their relationship with Jesus.

---

464 Jhn. 14:29

Appendix I

"Elohim" Is a Title, Not a Name

The Hebrew word "Elohim," unlike "JEHOVAH," is used as a title or as a reference to a being that is a deity; it is not a name. God never uses "Elohim" as His name. We read in the Book of Exodus that "God the Father" intentionally uses "Elohim" in the Book of Genesis to conceal His name. In Exodus 6:3, "God the Father" says, when the added phrase is removed, that "I appeared unto Abraham, unto Isaac, and unto Jacob, by God Almighty, but by my name JEHOVAH was I not known to them." Thus, "God the Father" says that He revealed Himself to Abraham, Isaac, and Jacob only by a title, "God Almighty." He intentionally does not reveal His name, "JEHOVAH," to them.

The KJV uses the Hebrew word "Elohim" 2,601 times in 2,247 verses in the OT. Of those 2,601 times, 218 of them occur in the Book of Genesis. Elohim is translated in different ways in the KJV: "God,"[465] "god,"[466] "gods,"[467] "mighty,"[468] "great,"[469] "judges,"[470] "judge,"[471] "goddess,"[472] "angels,"[473] "exceeding,"[474] and "godly."[475] Whether "Elohim" is translated as God, gods, goddess, etc., depends on the context. But, regardless of context, "Elohim" is never used as the name of God.

"Elohim" is a common noun, not a proper noun.[476] Hence, "Elohim" refers to God by His title, not by His name. "Elohim" is the plural of the Hebrew word "'ĕlôahh" (Elo'ah). It means:

> *gods in the ordinary sense; but specifically used (in the plural thus, especially*

---

465 Gen. 1:1, Exo. 2:24
466 Exo. 7:1, 1 Kin 11:33, Dan. 1:2
467 Gen. 3:5, 31:30; Exo. 20:3; Psa. 96:4
468 Gen. 23:6, Exo. 9:28
469 Gen. 30:8, 1 Sam. 14:15
470 Exo. 21:6, Exo. 22:8, Exo. 22:9
471 1 Sam. 2:25
472 1 Kin. 11:5
473 Psa. 8:5
474 Jon. 3:3
475 Mal. 2:15
476 Merriam-Webster.com Dictionary, s.v. "proper noun," accessed June 2, 2022, https://www.merriam-webster.com/dictionary/proper%20noun.

with the article) of the supreme God; occasionally applied by way of deference to magistrates; and sometimes as a superlative: - angels, X exceeding, God (gods) (-dess, -ly), X (very) great, judges, X mighty.[477]

"Elohim" is used in the KJV as plural, or singular, depending on its use: generically or specifically. "Elo'ah," in the singular common noun form, appears first in Deuteronomy 32:15, and it is used 57 times in 56 verses in the KJV. Another Hebrew word with a similar attribute is "har." "Har" can be both plural and singular, depending on the context. In Psalms 121:1, "har" is translated as "hills." Yet, in Isaiah 2:2, "har" is translated as "mountain" and "mountains." And, in Daniel 9:6, it is translated as "mountain. The number is determined by the context, not the spelling.

If we make the analogy that "Elohim" is to god as pastors is to pastor, then "pastors" is considered singular and not necessarily capitalized when used to refer to your specific pastor—aside from that it is spelled in the plural. Conversely, "pastors" is not capitalized and plural when used generically to refer to pastors, in general. Hence, "Elohim" is always singular and not necessarily capitalized when referring to a specific god in the

---

[477] Strong's Concordance H430

KJV. For example, we note that "Elohim" is singular and not capitalized when it refers to specific false gods in 1 Kings 11:33.

> *(1 Kin. 11:33) Because that they have forsaken me, and have worshipped Ashtoreth the goddess of the Zidonians, Chemosh the god of the Moabites, and Milcom the god of the children of Ammon, and have not walked in my ways, to do that which is right in mine eyes, and to keep my statutes and my judgments, as did David his father.*

In the above verse, "Elohim" is in the singular and not capitalized when referring to "the goddess of the Zidonians," to "the god of the Moabites," and to "the god of the children of Ammon." Likewise, in Daniel 1:2, we read that "the Lord gave Jehoiakim king of Judah into his hand, with part of the vessels of the house of God (Elohim): which he carried into the land of Shinar to the house of his god (Elohim); and he brought the vessels into the treasure house of his god (Elohim)." The first "Elohim" refers to the God of Abraham, Isaac, and Jacob. Therefore, it is capitalized. However, the second and third "Elohim" is singular and not capitalized because they do not refer to the God of Abraham, Isaac, and Jacob—they refer to the god of the Babylonians.

From these examples, we see that the singular form of "Elohim" can refer to more than just the God of Abraham, Isaac, and Jacob. However, when "Elohim" refers to the God of Abraham, Isaac, and Jacob, "Elohim" is singular and capitalized.

"Elohim" is, however, translated as "gods" five times in the KJV of Genesis. And, each time, except the first time, it refers to false gods.[478] The first time "Elohim" is translated as "gods" is in Genesis 3:5, when the serpent tells Eve that, "For God doth know that in the day ye eat thereof, then your eyes shall be opened, and ye shall be as gods, knowing good and evil." In this statement to Eve, the translators of the KJV are acknowledging, knowingly or unknowingly, that the serpent knew about the existence of the "Trinity." Otherwise, they would have translated "Elohim" as "God," as they had before.

Other translations did not translate the second "Elohim" in this sentence as "gods," they translated it as "God." The New International Version (NIV) of the Bible translated Genesis 3:5 as: "For God knows that when you eat from it your eyes will be opened, and you will be like God, knowing good and evil." The New American Standard Bible (ASB) translated Genesis 3:5 as: "For God

---

478 Gen. 3:5, 31:30, 31:32, 35:2, 35:4

knows that in the day you eat from it your eyes will be opened, and you will be like God, knowing good and evil." And, the New King James Version (NKJV) of the Bible translated Genesis 3:5 as: "For God knows that in the day you eat of it your eyes will be opened, and you will be like God, knowing good and evil."

Notwithstanding the KJV and the other aforementioned translations of this verse, I believe that the most accurate translation is: "For God doth know that in the day ye eat thereof, then your eyes shall be opened, and ye shall be as Gods, knowing good and evil." Thus, I would capitalize the plural "Gods" to show that it refers back to the Trinity. I believe that by not capitalizing "gods," the KJV is implying that the serpent is referring to false gods, not the Trinity. However, I believe that Satan is referring to the Trinity. I believe this because: (1) The Trinity exists in the beginning; (2) Satan is operating within the serpent, and Satan knows that the Trinity exists; and, (3) Each person in the Trinity: the Father, the Son, and the Holy Spirit, knew good and evil.

With the aforementioned in mind, we note that the KJV does not reveal the name of the God that speaks, or commands, creation into existence by repeatedly saying, "Let there be" in Genesis chapter 1. Neither does the KJV reveal the name of the "the Spirit of God [that] moved upon the face of the waters"[479] in chapter 1. However, the God in Genesis chapters 2 and 3: (1) "formed man of the dust of the ground, and breathed into his nostrils the breath of life"; (2) "commanded the man, saying, Of every tree of the garden thou mayest freely eat: But of the tree of the knowledge of good and evil, thou shalt not eat of it: for in the day that thou eatest thereof thou shalt surely die"; (3) made "coats of skins, and clothed" Adam and Eve; and, (4) this God is named "JHWH," or JEHOVAH. I also believe that this God is God the Son, Jesus, and He is the only God of the Trinity that Abraham, Isaac, and Jacob knew by name.

---

[479] Gen. 1:2

Appendix II

Other Hebrew Words Translated as "Vision"

Besides the Hebrew word "הַמַּחֲזֶה" (makh-az-eh'), there are five other Hebrew words that are translated as "vision" sixty more times in fifty-eight verses in the KJV. More specifically, the Hebrew word "הָמַּרְאָה" (mar'âh) occurs eleven times in ten verses, but it is translated as "vision" ten times in nine verses. In these cases, it means vision as a mode of revelation.[480]

The second Hebrew word is "חָזוֹן" (châzôn), and it occurs thirty-five times in thirty-four verses. The word means vision (in ecstatic state), (in night),

---

480 Brown-Driver-Briggs, H4759

vision, oracle, prophecy (divine communication), vision (as title of book of prophecy).[481]

The third Hebrew word translated as "vision" is "וְחִזָּיוֹן" (chizzâyôn), and it occurs nine times in nine verses. It means vision (in the ecstatic state), valley of vision (perhaps figuratively of Jerusalem or Hinnom), vision (in the night), vision, oracle, prophecy (in divine communication).[482]

The fourth Hebrew word is "תָזוּת" (châzûth), and it occurs five times in five verses. It means vision, conspicuousness, vision, oracle of a prophet, agreement, conspicuousness in appearance.[483]

The last Hebrew word is "הָרֹאֶה" (rô'eh), and it occurs six times in six verses. But it is translated as "vision" only once in one verse. It means seer, prophet (prophetic) vision.[484] Each of these Hebrew words is chosen in their corresponding Scriptures to convey a specific meaning. Thus, the choice of the Hebrew word in Genesis 15:1 is meant to convey the very great happiness that Jesus brought to Abram in this vision.

---

481 Brown-Driver-Briggs, H2377
482 Brown-Driver-Briggs, H2384
483 Brown-Driver-Briggs, H2380
484 Brown-Driver-Briggs, H7203

Appendix III

The Symbolism of Heifers in the Bible

The Hebrew word that the KJV translated as "heifer" in Genesis 15:9 is "הָעֶגְלָ" (eg-law').[485] This Hebrew is used fourteen times in thirteen OT verses: once in Genesis 15:9, four times in Deuteronomy, once in Judges, once in 1 Samuel, twice in Isaiah, three times in Jeremiah, and twice in Hosea. However, the English word "heifer" also appears in the Book of Numbers chapter 19, but the Hebrew word "הָעֶגְלָ" (eg-law') does not appear. Instead, the KJV reads "red heifer without spot, wherein is no blemish, and upon which never came yoke:"[486] The red heifer (Hebrew: הָפָרָה אֲדֻמָּה; para adumma),

---

485 Strong's Concordance H5697
486 Num. 19:2

"a female bovine which never been pregnant or milked or yoked, also known as the red cow, was a cow brought to the priests as a sacrifice according to the Torah, and its ashes were used for the ritual purification of Tum'at HaMet ("the impurity of the dead"), that is, an Israelite who had come into contact with a corpse."[487] These details are consistent with what we read in the Book of Deuteronomy chapter 21.

The following discusses how this Hebrew word is used in verses other than Genesis 15:9.

1. In Deuteronomy, the Hebrew word "עֶגְלָה" (eg-law') appears three times, and it is "heifer." The "heifer" in this chapter is used for the atonement for unsolved murders. In Deuteronomy 21:1, we read that when someone is "found slain in the land which the LORD thy God giveth thee to possess it, lying in the field, and it be not known who hath slain him," the elders of the city closest to where the body is found[488] are to "bring down the heifer unto a rough valley, which is neither eared nor sown, and

---

487 "Red Heifer." DBpedia. Accessed June 9, 2022. https://dbpedia.org/page/Red_heifer.
488 Deu. 21:2–3

shall strike off the heifer's neck there in the valley."[489]

"And the priests the sons of Levi shall come near; for them the LORD thy God hath chosen to minister unto him, and to bless in the name of the LORD; and by their word shall every controversy and every stroke be tried: And all the elders of that city, that are next unto the slain man, shall wash their hands over the heifer that is beheaded in the valley: And they shall answer and say, Our hands have not shed this blood, neither have our eyes seen it."[490] "Be merciful, O LORD, unto thy people Israel, whom thou hast redeemed, and lay not innocent blood unto thy people of Israel's charge. And the blood shall be forgiven them. So shalt thou put away the guilt of innocent blood from among you, when thou shalt do that which is right in the sight of the LORD."[491]

This purpose is reminiscent of Genesis 4:8 when "Cain talked with Abel his brother: and it came to pass, when they were in the field, that Cain rose up against Abel

---

489 Deu. 21:4
490 Deu. 21:5–7
491 Deu. 21:8–9

his brother, and slew him." Afterward, the LORD "said unto Cain, Where is Abel thy brother? And he said, I know not: Am I my brother's keeper? And he said, What hast thou done? the voice of thy brother's blood crieth unto me from the ground. And now art thou cursed from the earth, which hath opened her mouth to receive thy brother's blood from thy hand."[492] Thus, we have the first murder that may have gone unsolved if it were not for the LORD, who knew that Cain committed the murder.

2. In Judges 14:18, the Hebrew word "הָעֶגְלָ" (eg-law') appears once. In this chapter, Samson refers to his Philistine wife, who revealed the secret of his riddle to the Philistines, as a "heifer." Because there is no mention of Samson fathering children by this Philistine woman, or her having any children, we may conclude that she is barren at the time when Samson calls her a "heifer." Thus, Samson is likely referring to her barrenness when he calls her a "heifer."

3. In 1 Samuel 16:2, the Hebrew word "הָעֶגְלָ" (eg-law') appears once. In this chapter, the LORD told Samuel to "take an heifer with

---

492 Gen. 4:9–11

thee, and say, I am come to sacrifice to the LORD."[493] This verse could refer back to Numbers chapter 19, or Deuteronomy chapter 21, or the heifer could be used as a "Peace Offering." It could not be a "Burnt Offering" because those offering only used males of the herd and flock. Moreover, it could not be a "Sin Offering" because no female from the herd is used in "Sin Offerings," and it could not be a "Trespass or Guilt" Offering because no animal from the herd could be used.

4. In Isaiah 7:21, the Hebrew word "הָעֵגֶל" (eg-law') appears twice. This verse uses a theme of a virgin conceiving or a damsel giving birth to her first child. In Isaiah 7:14, we read that "the Lord himself shall give you a sign; Behold, a virgin shall conceive, and bear a son, and shall call his name Immanuel." Likewise, we read in Isaiah 7:21–22 that "it shall come to pass in that day, that a man shall nourish a young cow, and two sheep; And it shall come to pass, for the abundance of milk that they shall give he shall eat butter: for butter and

---

493 1 Sam. 16:2

honey shall every one eat that is left in the land."[494]

We note that the KJV translates the Hebrew word "הָעֶגְלָ" as "cow" in Isaiah 7:21, but it is translated as "heifer" in Genesis 15:9. The thought of a "cow" giving milk does not fit the theme of a virgin one day conceiving in Isaiah 7:14. However, the thought of a heifer one day giving milk fits better the theme of a virgin giving birth one day. This is because a virgin and a heifer are both childless, and they can produce milk.

A second reason to question the translation of the Hebrew word "הָעֶגְלָ" to "cow" is that of the thirteen verses that contain this Hebrew word, it is only translated as "cow" once. In all the other twelve verses, "הָעֶגְלָ" is translated as "heifer" in eleven of those verses and "calves" once. Thus, "heifer" does appear to be the most consistent translation of this Hebrew word.

5. The next time we read of a heifer in the KJV is in Isaiah 15:5. In this verse, we read, "My heart shall cry out for Moab; his fugitives shall flee unto Zoar, an heifer of three

---

494 Isa. 7:21–22

years old."[495] Similarly, Jeremiah 48:34 reads, "From the cry of Heshbon even unto Elealeh, and even unto Jahaz, have they uttered their voice, from Zoar even unto Horonaim, as an heifer of three years old."[496]

6. In Jeremiah 50:11, we read, "Because ye were glad, because ye rejoiced, O ye destroyers of mine heritage, because ye are grown fat as the heifer at grass, and bellow as bulls." We find a clue to the meaning of this Scripture in the verses that immediately follow, Jeremiah 50:12–13. These two verses read, "Your mother shall be sore confounded; she that bare you shall be ashamed: behold, the hindermost of the nations shall be a wilderness, a dry land, and a desert. Because of the wrath of the LORD it shall not be inhabited, but it shall be wholly desolate: every one that goeth by Babylon shall be astonished, and hiss at all her plagues."[497] In these two verses, we see references to conditions that reflect barrenness: wilderness, dry land, desert, and not to be inhabited. Thus, a heifer that has

---

495 Isa. 15:5
496 Jer. 48:34
497 Jer. 50:12–13

grown fat eating grass is a symbol of the nation of Babylon growing in the territory, but whose land will ultimately be left "a wilderness, a dry land, and a desert"[498] that "shall not be inhabited."[499]

7. In Hosea 10:5, the verse reads, "The inhabitants of Samaria shall fear because of the calves of Bethaven: for the people thereof shall mourn over it, and the priests thereof that rejoiced on it, for the glory thereof, because it is departed from it." In this verse, "הָעֲגָל" is translated in the KJV as "calves."

The Prophetic Meaning of the Heifer
The heifer points to the barren "New Covenant" and the unfulfilled "Covenant of Redemption." The Book of Hebrews talks about the unfulfillment of "the ashes of an heifer sprinkling the unclean, sanctifieth to the purifying of the flesh: How much more shall the blood of Christ, who through the eternal Spirit offered himself without spot to God, purge your conscience from dead works to serve the living God?"[500] Heifers are used to cleanse those that touched the dead, and to seek mercy and forgiveness from the LORD for

---

498 Jer. 50:12
499 Jer. 50:13
500 Heb. 9:13–14

unsolved murders. We note that a "red heifer" is used to cleanse those that touched the dead.

Therefore, the heifer points to the fulfillment of the "Covenant of Redemption," the "New Covenant," and the general resurrection of the dead saints that die before the coming of Jesus in the NT. Consequently, the heifer, which represents the barren Sarai, points to the day that the "Old Covenant" is established at Mount Sinai.

This symbolic heifer, however, will one day bear a symbolic male calf. In that day, the heifer will transform into a symbolic cow, and it will represent Sarah. And, accordingly, the symbolic male calf will represent Isaac and points to the day of the fulfillment of the "Covenant of Redemption," the general resurrection of the dead saints, and the establishment of the "New Covenant."

Index of Questions

Did Abraham, Isaac, and Jacob know God the Father's Name? 67

Did Abram's descendants ever possess the entire Promised Land? 203

Did all of Abraham's descendants receive "rights of sonship."? 82

Does the New Testament make a distinction between "Made" and "Created"? 23

How did Jesus fulfill the Covenant of Redemption? 30

How long were the Children of Israel in Egypt? 167

Is the God in Genesis Chapter 1 different from the God in Genesis chapter 2? 18

Is Jesus the only person of the Trinity that mankind, at any time, has seen or touched? . 25

On what were the requirements for the "rights of sonship" based? 83

What are evil people? 64

What are the "Appointed Days" of the LORD?. 84

What do the sacrificial animals in Genesis chapter 15 represent? 121

What does the oil in the lamp of the ten virgins represent? 133

What event marked the end of the 70-week prophecy in Daniel chapter 9? 188

What is an enemy? 64

What is God's name? 16

What is the difference between LORD, Lord, and lord in the Bible? 16

What is the Great Commission? 39

What is the meaning of "Elohim" in the Bible? 17

What is the symbolism of the Smoking Furnace and Burning Lamp? 191

What terms refer to young-unbred sheep, goats, and cattle?... 96

What were the boundaries of the Promised Land?... 203

When and to whom did God the Father first reveal His Name to?... 75

When did the 400 years identified in Genesis chapter 15 begin and end? 163

When is the Sabbath first introduced in the Bible?.. 26

Where did the ritual-substitutional sacrifice of a male lamb without blemish begin? 30

Where is the word "vision" first used in the Bible?.. 35

Who are the covenanters of the Covenant of Redemption? 28

Why did Peter tell the crowd to "be baptized every one of you in the name of Jesus Christ," instead of using the "Great Commission" formulary? 73

Why didn't Abram participate in the cutting of the covenant? 13

www.ingramcontent.com/pod-product-compliance
Lightning Source LLC
Chambersburg PA
CBHW061253110426
42742CB00012BA/1904